P9-DDI-216

Other Books by Calvin Miller

BURNING BUSHES AND MOON WALKS
GUARDIANS OF THE SINGREALE
A HUNGER FOR MEANING
IF THIS BE LOVE
ONCE UPON A TREE
THE PHILIPPIAN FRAGMENT
POEMS OF PROTEST AND FAITH
THE SINGER TRILOGY
THE SINGER
THE SONG
THE FINALE
SIXTEEN DAYS ON A CHURCH CALENDAR
STAR RIDERS OF REN
THE TABLE OF INWARDNESS
THE TASTE OF JOY
TRANSCENDENTAL HESITATION
THE VALIANT PAPERS
A VIEW FROM THE FIELDS
WAR OF THE MOONRHYMES

CALVIN MILLER
author of *The Singer*

THE TABLE OF INWARDNESS

INTER-VARSITY PRESS
DOWNERS GROVE
ILLINOIS 60515

InterVarsity Press is the book-publishing division of Inter-Varsity Christian Fellowship, a student movement active on campus at hundreds of universities, colleges and schools of nursing. For information about local and regional activities, write IVCF, 233 Langdon St., Madison, WI 53703.

Distributed in Canada through InterVarsity Press, 860 Denison St., Unit 3, Markham, Ontario L3R 4H1, Canada.

Acknowledgment is made for permission to quote from the following:

"Prayer . . . The Priority!" by Jack Taylor from The Future Church, compiled by Ralph W. Neighbour, Jr. (Nashville: Broadman Press, 1980), p. 79. All rights reserved. Used by permission.

Louis Evely, That Man Is You, translated by Edmond Bonin. Copyright © 1963. Used by permission of Paulist Press.

Giles Fletcher, "He Is," reprinted from Dawnings: Finding God's Light in the Darkness. Edited by Phyllis Hobe. Copyright © 1981 by Guideposts Associates, Inc., Carmel, New York 10512.

Earl D. Radmacher, You and Your Thoughts. Used by permission.

Scripture quotations from the Revised Standard Version of the Bible, copyrighted 1946, 1952, © 1971, 1973.

Paul E. Billheimer, Don't Waste Your Sorrows. Copyright 1977. Used by permission of Christian Literature Crusade, Inc.

Cover photograph: Robert McKendrick

ISBN 0-87784-832-7

Printed in the United States of America

Library of Congress Cataloging in Publication Data

Miller, Calvin.
The table of inwardness.

Includes bibliographical references.
1. Spiritual life—Baptist authors. I. Title.
BV4501.2.M4726 1984 248.4'861 84-9134
ISBN 0-87784-832-7

---

19 18 17 16 15 14 13 12 11 10 9 8 7 6 5 4 3 2 1
98 97 96 95 94 93 92 91 90 89 88 87 86 85 84

The Table

In this secluded place I meet
 a King.
He comes alone to drink
 reality
With me. Sometimes we talk, sometimes
 we sit
And sip a life that passes by the
 crowd
As inwardness is born—
 a felted thing
Of power—a commonality—
A union where unmended hopes
 are knit
Where silence roars as quiet
 sings aloud.
Oh Christ, I love it here!
 It is our place.
Speak Lord or not. Touch me
 or not. Show then
Your will or bid me wait in
 patient grace.
Fill all my hungry need
 with joy again.
With simple loaves of bread and chaliced wine
Heaven, earth and all of God are mine.

When you are able to create a lonely place in the middle of your actions and concerns, your successes and failures slowly can lose some of their power over you.

Henri J. M. Nouwen

While in the race to save our face, why not conquer inner space?

Anonymous

GALILEO: I'm not a theologian: I'm a mathematician.
SAGREDO: You are a human being! [Almost shouting]: Where is God in your system of the universe?
GALILEO: Within ourselves. Or—nowhere.

Bertolt Brecht

I
The Issue of Inwardness

WE SHRINK TO STEP across the threshold to ourselves. We do not hesitate to stick our hands into the throng and shake a thousand others. But turning from others, we face our inner self with fear. Why?

Who can tell all the reasons? Inwardness seems a kind of nakedness and soul exposure. Self simpers where none can see, outwardly pretending to be gallant and noble. Inwardly, it is critical of others while on the outside it smiles and flatters. Inward it cries and outward plays the clown.

The journey inward is painful. Remember Hamlet before his mother; "Come, come, and sit you down, you shall not budge! You go not till I set you up a glass where you may see the inmost part of you."[1] The young prince forces his mother to look at her true self hidden at the center of her being. The question is, what did Gertrude see? What sort of inner self does the glass reflect?

In many Bible passages (such as Lk 13:3 or Acts 2:38) there

is the call for us to come to God by way of repentance. Repentance? The word stops our very hearts with heaviness for it calls for a bold disclosure of our inward selves to our loving Father. Yet it is more. In repentance we stand with God as, together, we look inward, and throw even the darkest issues of ourselves beneath his certain light.

I remember that night so long ago when, as a child, I asked the living Christ to enter my life. Suddenly, even as a child, I knew the pain of Hamlet's reflecting glass. But the pain soon left and in its place a radiant reality was born.

I remember the frustration of trying to tell my friends about the inward Christ who had replaced my guilt and bad feelings with his glorious self. I could tell by the way they looked that they could not understand. I wanted everyone to know. I tried to tell my family, but they had the same quizzical expressions. The Christ inside me was magnificent but could not be explained to anyone's satisfaction. I could not make him big enough to fit the inner glory that I felt, and the world beyond me could not make him little enough to fit in its small understanding.

At a strikingly early age I learned that life in Christ is so inward it cannot be externalized completely. The historical facts surrounding Christ are clear. Certainly the theological truths are sure. Yet the reality of Jesus is always a matter of the heart. The fullness of his great love and salvation live beyond the portals of our most private selves. There alone we meet him.

Writing this introduction to inwardness is a task that has all the same frustrations I felt as a child. How can I tell you? How shall I define it? Inwardness defies all laws of space and time, and endows us with a life and destiny greater than our own. What we contain is more than what we are. It is heaven, immeasurable, love without dimensions: all in the confines of a fleshly frame. It is the fullness of purpose, without which there is no great purpose.

Alan Watts spoke of "the very center of the very center." His daughter once complained that she could see only the outside of things. Since they were eating grapes at the time, Watts grabbed a knife and cut a grape in half. But to his daughter, who now felt she saw the inside of a grape, he said, "This is not the inside of the inside. It is only the outside of the inside." To see the "inside of the inside" he would have to cut the half grape into quarters, which he did only to seal the "inside of the inside" into eighths. Whenever Watts attempted to open the center of the grape, he only succeeded in creating new "outsides" and driving the "inside" further "in."

The point is made! Discussing inwardness does not define it and exposing it is impossible. We cannot ever really locate it: does it reside in the mind or in the heart? What is the difference between the two? Evangelicals, from their first experiences in faith, teach their children to "invite Jesus into their hearts." Those same children are taught to sing:

Into my heart, into my heart,
Come into my heart, Lord Jesus.
Come in today. Come in to stay.
Come into my heart, Lord Jesus.

There are a thousand other such songs and prayers. Some Christians distrust the kind of faith that emphasizes thinking and logic at the expense of feeling. We are like the Tin Man in *The Wizard of Oz,* who believed all his problems would be solved if he only had a heart.

In actuality, the mind and heart are both one in purposes of faith. But inwardness which produces true spiritual vitality is dependent on both. No wonder Moses in the Shema asked Israel to love the Lord God with all of the heart, soul and mind (Deut 6:5). And Paul encouraged the Philippians to let the mind of Christ indwell their own (Phil 2:5). Such invitations do not divide inwardness between heart and brain. Thought and emotions are both parts of the whole. An inwardness that only feels may be warm but intellectually retarded. One that thinks but doesn't feel is void of hope and compassion.

Breaking the Bonds

With true inwardness God declares himself without the hard sell. Inwardness is the great and silent witness to the magnificence of God. Evangelism is the trumpet that calls the lost to Christ, but inwardness waves in silence: an unseen banner above the heart of the believer.

I used to wonder why Francis of Assisi or Theresa of Avilà or Juan de Cruz never gave the world a scheme of witnessing, a so-called plan of salvation. But Theresa spoke for God out of her appetite for him. Her life held the proclamation of inner reality. Francis of Assisi did not lead people to Jesus as modern evangelists do. But he hungered to be an "instrument of God's peace," and from his hunger was born an affair of heart that awakened his world to the reality of Christ.

Recently, in Avilà, I stood before that narrow, low-ceilinged cell where Theresa and Juan de Cruz prayed. In that cell, their inner life became so vibrant that it is said they levitated, rising against gravity toward the heaven-enthroned Christ they adored. Whether or not they actually rose from the floor is not central. What is important is that they nurtured an inner life so strong it broke the mental tethers that bound them to the world at hand. The cords of ordinary living are severed in Christ. Dull gravity cannot bind us to this earth, for heaven indwells us.

In contrast, when *Jonathan Livingston Seagull* was being filmed, the cameras in some shots focused on gulls in flight. But the gulls were really tied to a perch with strings. They only appeared to be free. Likewise, so many of us are tied to earthly concerns while we give the appearance of spiritual freedom. How thick are the cords that bind us to Christian reputation! Outward appearance fastens us to our own false needs for approval. I think of how often, as pastor, I have acted as people expected me to. Only the journey inward could release me from the strings of religious propriety. On the inward journey I meet him and am delivered from the bondage of outward expectation.

Outwardness and inwardness are the poles of spirituality as north and south are poles of the earth's geography. Outwardness consists of observable qualities of faith. Outwardness bandages the suffering in the clear sight of all who will behold compassion. It goes to church, lifts the communion wafer, holds hymnals, bends knees, traces crosses in the air. It drops coins in offering boxes, posts its public pledges, listens, sermonizes, sings, prays, witnesses, and works its way from prison to hospital.

Outwardness is good but easily spoiled. A few pats on the back can wean it from its first love and draw it toward self-interest. Soon outwardness, which first served Christ alone, finds ways to serve itself *while* it serves Christ. At last it moves away from Christ altogether and finds a godlike glory in its own interests.

There are many examples of outwardness gone bad. Outwardness often becomes an unending spiritual performance that lasts until the actor drops from empty exhaustion. A friend of mine at first found pleasure in his attempts to please his congregation. Later those same desires nearly drove him mad because no matter how hard he tried nothing he did pleased them. His sermons went flat. His programs fizzled. His leadership was questioned. Finally, his own failures brought him to the edge of insanity, and he resigned his pastorate. Only then could he admit that the crushing circumstances had driven him to inwardness beyond the outward show. His own inadequacy, at last, brought life to what had been spiritual pretense.

Christ strongly denounced the outwardness divorced from inwardness that he found in the Pharisees. The word *hypocrite,* which Christ often applied to the Pharisees, refers to an actor's mask. The Pharisees dressed themselves as God's champions while keeping their own visibility a first priority.

> They bind heavy burdens, hard to bear, and lay them on men's shoulders; but they themselves will not move them with their finger. They do all their deeds to be seen by men; for they make their phylacteries broad and their fringes long, and they love the place of honor at feasts and the best seats in the synagogues, and salutations in the market places and being called rabbi by men. (Mt 23:4-7)

The Pharisees really loved their showy spirituality.

Later in Matthew 23 Jesus pronounced seven woes on their outwardness that had degenerated into spiritual narcissism. Listen to Christ's condemnations of their "holy" exhibitionism: "For a pretense you make long prayers" (Mt 23:14). Christ criticized them for evangelism that only brought their converts to the captivity of their own suffocating, spiritual showiness (Mt 24:15). Their passion for orthodoxy shut God out of the central areas of their faith (Mt 23:16-22). They kept laws but by-passed compassion (Mt 23:23). Outwardly they were a clean cup that inside was germ infested (Mt 23:25). They were a mausoleum with a fancy front concealing inner decay (Mt 23:27). Their outwardness honored traditions, but killed current truth (Mt 23:29-36).

I do not believe that the Jewish establishment saw itself as selfish or exhibitionist. The Pharisees thought they were defenders of Mosaic law and purifiers of national morality. They were ministers of religion and keepers of truth. Their robes marked them as professionals; they were not phony. Their phylacteries may have been large, but they contained the holy law and were worn by holy men. This was not merely their opinion. In general all those they served thought the same. To those who respected the Pharisees, Jesus' words must have sounded unjustifiably critical.

Hypocrisy cannot define the instant of its birth. It is nurtured when self-interest and God's interest pass close enough that one deed serves both: a pat on the back for self-sacrifice. Herein lies the great captivity of the modern church. We cannot measure how much of our worship is for God and how much is for ourselves. This has been one of my primary concerns as a pastor. I believe the worship of our church is generally offered to Christ, but I often turn to find I have only used his name to sanctify my own. I want to please Christ, and yet I am so easily diverted from his pleasure to mine by the simple phrase: "That was a fine sermon, pastor!" I am drawn to pursue the compliment rather than the Christ.

Let me be clear. Outwardness is as important as inwardness and either may be phony or real. We need to remember that the same Jesus who said, "Beware of practicing your piety before men in order to be seen by them" (Mt 6:1) also said, "Every one who acknowledges me before men, I also will acknowledge before my Father" (Mt 10:32).

Outwardness has for its greatest strength and greatest weakness the same thing: visibility. Likewise the strength and weakness of inwardness is the same: invisibility. Inwardness draws us to that unseen reality. But it may sin secretly by dividing its own intent, scheming to make life better for both God and the worshiper at once.

We are the keepers of inwardness and we tend it alone. Our guardianship is utterly crucial, since out of the heart come "the issues of life" (Prov 4:23 KJV). As someone once pointed out, we are like a ripe fruit which, when squeezed, displays its real contents. According to Jesus, being kosher isn't crucial. It's not what goes into our mouths—what we eat or drink—but what comes out of our hearts that defiles us (Mt 15:11). What comes out shows our inner substance: "As a man thinketh in his heart so is he" (Prov 23:7 KJV). God focuses his attention on our inwardness. "Man looks on the outward appearance, but the LORD looks on the heart" (1 Sam 16:7).

My hunger for God as a youth kept me looking for evidence of the reality of God. I wanted him to speak audibly—even just one word—so I could be sure of his existence. If only he would manifest himself for one minute, I would be content, concrete evidence in hand. But my youthful searchings always stopped at the surface of faith until I learned that Christ must be found inside.

In search of God I often take
My ordered world apart
To learn that when my search was done
I found him at my very heart.[2]

Inwardness is the place where the believer and his Lord meet. In this book, I will speak of the heart as the place of rendezvous. In this small meeting place exists the inwardness which we consider.

Three Paradoxes

Our work will be complicated by three paradoxes. The first puzzle is the aloneness-is-presence paradox. One writer says, "No individual's prayer life will be greater than the quality of his regular time set aside to meet God alone."[3] Inner silence must be established, or we cannot hear the indwelling Christ with whom we desire to speak. I will deal with this silence in a later chapter, but for now I must say that it is established by certain premeditative disciplines that clear away the debris and noise of life.

Inner silence is easiest to achieve in a place of outer silence. This is the prayer closet that Jesus spoke of in Matthew 6. Here we shut out as much human intercourse as possible. Yet, we are never to pursue inwardness. We are to pursue Christ. There is no power in meditative systems that clear the heart but cannot refill it with substance. In my years of studying Eastern religions, I discovered that many devotees of yoga cleanse their minds but leave them empty. Soon their minds refill with the same sort of congestion which had just been swept away.

Inwardness seeks someone to preside over the clean and the quiet. When Christ comes in, we have provided ourselves an inner worship that is proper. We are not alone with quietness but with him. Inwardness is a reigning presence, and a quiet friend—a person, not a concept. The world may regard this as loneliness. But the paradox is set; aloneness is the presence.

The second paradox in seeking an understanding of inwardness is that retreat is advancement. To some who desire inwardness, time alone with God may not seem to yield anything practical in their personal plans or career. So why spend time with God when so many things have to be done?

When Malcolm Muggeridge visited the monastery at Nunraw, Scotland, he expected to find a group of men who had little to do with the world of commerce. What he discovered was that real men of prayer may undergird national and international communication because their retreat gives them unbroken touch with him who holds the very universe in his hand.

When we speak of praying monks, we formalize prayer as a retreat. Prayer must have that dimension, to be sure. But later in this book we will also speak of continuing prayer which does not interrupt our daily life, but marches to accompany it. Brother Lawrence said, "The time of business does not differ with me from the time of prayer: and in the noise and clatter of my kitchen, while several persons are at the same time calling for different things, I possess God as if I were upon my knees at the blessed sacrament."[4]

Still, formal retreat is necessary if we would find him, if we want our time with him to be free of the clatter of life in the laundry or office. Brother Lawrence would no doubt confess that his kitchen prayers proceeded from the base he gave them in his more quiet and solitary moments. Unless we have time set aside to be with God, the other hours committed to our schedules will be ill-used. Christians are prone to ignore times of retreat because ministering seems more important: doing seems better than praying. But prayer is doing. Retreat is not idleness; it is a rigorous discipline of the inner self. We must not let even ministry to others supplant it. Mother Teresa of Calcutta said, "Pray for me that I not loosen my grip on the hands of Jesus even under the guise of ministry to the poor."[5] No, retreat is advancement; prayer, even extended prayer, is a practical way to spend time, especially for the busy. Martin Luther's attitude was, "I have so many things to do today, I dare not ignore my time with God."

The third paradox is that beyond is within. Cosmic is the name of Christ. The heavens do declare the glory of God (Ps 19:1), yet the Christ who strides the galaxies gathers at a quiet communion with our selves. We do not contain all the fullness of God for we are too small for that, but we are possessed by a transgalactic Omnipotence who comes to indwell us.

Our problem is this: we usually discover him within some denominational or Christian ghetto. We meet him in a province and, having caught some little view, we paint him in smaller strokes. The Lion of Judah is reduced to something kittenish because our understanding cannot, at first, write larger definitions.

In a sense, Jesus' own description of himself was too great for the Jewish establishment of his day. "Before Abraham was, I am," he said (Jn 8:58). "I am the living bread which came down from heaven" (Jn 6:51). "Do you think that I cannot appeal to my Father, and he will at once send me more than twelve legions of angels?" he declared triumphantly (Mt 26:53). "They will see the Son of Man coming in clouds with great power and glory" (Mk 13:26). Statements like these interrupt the ordinary structures of small hearts. Christ is the dynamic beyond that dwells within.

Three Dangers

There are three dangers ahead of us as we seek to know him in inner fullness. First, the desire to go deeper breeds its own addiction and may keep us from seeing the needs of our world. Ministry to others accompanies depth of spirit. When the pursuit of the inner Christ obscures the outer world of lostness and human hurt, our hunger of heart is a perversion. Jesus said unless we have ministered to those about us we have not ministered to him (Mt 25:44-45). This issue requires a delicate balance. We must see with bifocal vision the Christ who is within us and the Christ who is beyond us. To lose view of either Christ is to live in our world as a stranger to God and man.

A second danger is that most will see our quest as otherworldly. "We are too heavenly minded to be much earthly good," they say. The only answer we can give is that we have entered a life that holds stock in the next world as it hungers to redeem this present one. We are not trying to get out of the pain and pressure of contemporary living. We are simply taking steps to infuse it with meaning. The present is but the narrow preface to the eternal. Our role is to do all we can to help the world see that if this age is all we own, we will shortly be disinherited. To ignore our own transience is folly.

The third danger is that we shall be trapped in the "sweet-Jesus" syndrome. The hymn writer is right—there's a sweetness in our communion with our Lord. How often the word *sweet* appears in our description of our understanding of Jesus: "Sweet little Jesus boy;" "There's a sweet, sweet spirit in this place;" "Swing low, sweet chariot;" "Sweet hour of prayer"! This high-calorie addiction often gets sticky and gums up ordinary worship. But most of all, it addicts us to the lovely *feeling* we hold for Jesus rather than to Jesus himself.

With these cautions in mind, we are ready to begin. There is an old Chinese proverb that says, "If you want to know what water is, a fish is the last one to ask." Perhaps people who possess true inwardness will not see themselves as authorities on the subject.

Fellowship with Christ is a table only for two—set in the wilderness. Inwardness is not a gaudy party but the meeting of lovers in the lonely desert of the human heart. There, where all life and fellowship can hold no more than two, we sit together and he speaks as much as we, and even when both of us say nothing there is our welded oneness. And suddenly we see we cannot be complete until his perfect presence joins with ours.

I must create a System or be enslav'd by another Man's.
William Blake

Let us look at ourselves if we can bear to, and see
what is becoming of us. First we must face
that unexpected revelation, striptease of our humanism.
Jean-Paul Sartre

When Soul and body feed, one sees
Their differing physiologies.
Firmness of apple, fluted shape
Of celery, or tight-skinned grape
I grind and mangle when I eat,
Then in dark, salt, internal heart,
Annihilate their natures by
The very act that makes them I.
C. S. Lewis

2
Barriers to the Inward Journey

WE ARE VESSELS. God created us to be receptacles of himself, but in spite of the Holy Spirit's readiness to invade our lives, most of us hold nothing. Our inner lives created by God to contain himself hold only little dreams.

Carl Jung believed that the central neurosis of our time was the absence of inwardness. Our worship as well as the content of popular books and sermons betray a lack of depth. "Christianity is best because it is the fastest way to personal gain." We serve Christ while we worship Narcissus. Our slick religious tabloids abound with articles like "God Saved My Business!" Books (and records and tapes) on Christian aerobics, Christian cosmetics and Christian diets abound. A medicine-show Christ attracts us to a gospel of prosperity.

Sometime ago a book entitled *I Prayed Myself Slim!* told the story of an obese Cinderella who had been trapped in her own body. In a fit of spirituality, she took her overweight condition to Christ, and he began to help her lose weight. Overnight she was transformed into a beautiful princess, desired by the most exciting bachelors in town. God had rescued her from her fate as a wallflower and cast her gloriously into the fast lane of life! Naturally, she gave all the credit to God.

Perhaps the young lady should have asked, "Does God want the credit?" The issue is not whether or not God can deliver us to our best selves, but whether or not God's main agenda is to create Cinderellas. In fact God wants us to glorify his Son and escape the prison of self. Yet a new Christian egotism insists that a Christianized self is an adequate center for life.

A vacuum is a depressurized space that longs to draw whatever substance it can into the void. The human spirit is just such a space within us that becomes a junk receptacle, filled with whatever is nearest.

Many years ago, someone gave me an antique wooden dynamite box made in the nineteenth century. For years I prized that box. It was meticulously constructed with mitered corners, and bore an ominous warning printed in bold red and black letters: "Danger Dynamite!" At one time the box had, indeed, been dangerous; its contents had to be handled gently. But the last time I saw it, the box was filled with common paraphernalia that could be found in any workroom. There's some force in the universe that doesn't like empty boxes! So when the emptiness is not filled by careful design, it becomes a catchall. The box is a parable of Christians in our time. Designed to bear the power of God, we are haphazardly filled with the trivia of our world.

Spiritual inwardness is a longing after Christ. It is a table set for us with food not prepared by human hands. The Host is there. He is ready. "Thou preparest a table before me . . ." (Ps 23:5). There are only two chairs at the table, and there we may delight to sit and sup with the Son of God.

The intrigue of the table in Psalm 23 has marked my life as

a pastor. The metaphor mixes itself in glory. The shepherd becomes the sheep and God becomes the shepherd. There is no flock. There are only two. The shepherd and his love walk alone and uninterrupted from the pleasant fields through the threatening chasm and back again. Their glory is not the path they walk but their togetherness.

And how do we come to the table in the wilderness? Exactly as we would to any other table—hungry. Our hunger is for him whom we really can never know fully in a group, no matter how religious that group is.

Do we not feel a certain reluctance to be there, alone with our Host who knows everything about us? Do we not feel repentance even as we sit at the table? Do we not desire to weep? Do we not feel emotion surging? Yes, but emotional feasting is not the reason we come to the table. We do not come to vent our emotion. We come to be with him. Deep feelings may be our response. Our fellowship with Christ, like all of life, may be marked by laughter and tears, but we meet with him because we need him and not because we need to laugh or to cry.

Yet what of those times when our enemies gather against us? There is no panic. With our Host we sit in quietness with food as rich as our relationship. Those who brandish weapons and make threatening advances do not understand how we can act as though we are secluded in some grotto. The marvelous truth is that there is a grotto! It is not carved with stone or shaped by events. It is a grotto of the heart. It is made of materials from another universe. For as real as the battlefield appears, true reality is measured another way.

As a child, I remember photographs of Americans landing on the beachheads in World War 2. If I place this lonely table into the violence of these beachheads, I catch a glimpse of Psalm 23 in a new way. Here, in the thick of terror and aggression, I yet may know the best reality: Jesus has taken up residence.

The Young Lions

Another battle rages, however, that is just as threatening to the table as any menacing enemy. This is our inner battle with sin. We are subject to a host of appetites that war against the hunger of the spirit. They prowl the wilderness like young lions in search of prey. They devour the meal laid for our pilgrimage and spoil the table.

Psychology speaks of "anality" regarding that phase of our childhood development when we are most concerned with elimination. Anality, say the psychologists, is always a reminder of our earthliness that rails against our idealism. Our bodies never let us forget that no matter how lofty our thinking or dreaming becomes, we are always tied to the gastric functions of life. We cannot both eat and be angels in this world. Every visionary has been tied to the "dish and pot," which Thomas à Becket called the "two extremities of man."

St. Paul reckoned with the old nature. He hungered for that perfect life that ended at glorification in a realm where we are finally set free of every lower definition. He cried that no matter how ideal his Christianity became, he was still shackled. He was unable to enjoy an uninterrupted face-to-face relationship with Christ. He found himself dealing, sometimes unsuccessfully, with fierce yet ordinary drives. His strong desire to please the Savior became snarled in demanding contradictions: "I find it to be a law that when I want to do right, evil lies close at hand. For I delight in the law of God, in my inmost self, but I see in my members another law at war with the law of my mind and making me captive to the law of sin which dwells in my members. Wretched man that I am! Who will deliver me from this body of death?" (Rom 7:21-24).

Obviously, the inner struggle is titanic. But there are valuable lessons to be learned. For one thing, this same continuous quarrel rages in every Christian. Our most determined efforts at personal reform do not last long. We win only as we achieve a constant walk with Christ. Human effort loses the fiber in its intention. Discipline is a matter of the inner reign of Christ. He will be victorious when he is allowed full sovereignty.

For Christ himself did not escape the battle. The Word became flesh and dwelt among us (Jn 1:14). He understood what it meant to be human in every category. In becoming a man, Christ shattered mere humanness as a barrier to inwardness. Becket was speaking purely physiologically when he called the "dish and pot" the extremities of life. Christ proved that spiritual life may indwell natural life. We are more than thinking, praying digestive tracts. We are worshiping persons.

The best way, then, to deal with sin is not to attempt reform but to adore the Savior. Winning over our lower nature is made positive by adoration. While we worship the enthroned and inner Christ, we cannot be intrigued by negative preoccupations with sin.

For generations much of the Christian church has foolishly sought to arrive at holiness by code. We have developed rigid ethical frameworks to protect our discipleship. But they have produced only frustrated disciples. "Spiritual" rule books are paper defenses. The trouble is they are never complete. Certain church covenants contain prohibitions against the sale and use of alcoholic beverages but never mention more contemporary evils of drug abuse or racial discrimination. These legalistic codes also usually say nothing about the less visible inward sins of jealousy or hatred that destroy our fellowship at the table.

Not only are rules beside the point, they set Christians in judgment over each other. A friend of mine once attended a church potluck dinner. She was standing in line behind a man who was smoking a cigarette. She said to him, "Where do you propose to snuff your tobacco in heaven?" To which the man with the cigarette replied, "In your coffee cup." Without rules, such judgments cannot pass between believers.

Legalism aborts relationships with both God and with others. Its focus is negative. The evil we seek to avoid grows, with concentration, into targets we cannot miss. Rules, instead of limiting our sin, define sin, rivet our attention to it and lead us to desire it. Worship, on the other hand, avoids all interest in sin, pointing our hearts and minds in a totally different direction.

Double Jeopardy of the West

Where does preconversion nature surface? In many areas. I will touch on four: sex, food, power and hurriedness.

Sexual desire is demanding and constant. It has influenced the history of the world. Initially, the church fathers were extremely zealous in their devotion to God, and their celibacy was only a by-product of that commitment. In time, celibacy became a legalism. There are extreme examples of this. Origen had himself castrated as a literal fulfillment of Matthew 19:12. It is better when devotion to Christ precedes the rule. St. Francis, for example, proclaimed he had taken a bride more beautiful than any offering of human companionship. The noble sacraments of holy orders enticed him to the life of celibacy. He was not following a rule but a Lover.

Liberated Christians in our day have taken the subject to press and made sex an open issue. Much of this new openness is a result of the sexual revolution that has characterized recent decades. At first, we spoke cautiously on the subject, seeking New Testament precedents. But some felt the church spoke too late. Others felt that late was better than never.

In a single century, observed Stuart Barton Babbage, we

have gone from a culture which talked openly of death and guardedly of sex to one which speaks guardedly about death and openly about sex. Sexuality has become a preoccupation with the arts. The golden phallus has risen in the idolatry of the West and a bumper sticker laments, "Remember when air was clean and sex was dirty?"

The saints demonstrate that the passion of the glands can be as great as that spiritual love which hungers after God. Elizabeth of Hungary, a thirteenth-century mystic, married a lusty crusader named Louis. Elizabeth's passion for Louis drove her to constant lust for him. Even in church she was driven by erotic desire. Merely seeing him festively arrayed at Mass, she fell under a great longing to kiss him. Her flights of romantic love so captured her mind that she often forgot she was in church. But this fierce yearning for Louis was only one aspect of a double madness. She was also passionate in her pursuit of the Holy God whom she desired with an equal ardor. She cried out to know the approval of Christ, greatly striving for his pleasure as well.

Louis left their young marriage feeling a spiritual obligation to go on a crusade. Elizabeth missed him with a love that caused a "boiling in her blood" along with desires "to kiss her husband with many kisses" and to embrace him in full love. But in his continued absence, she found the inner and powerful presence of Christ began to motivate her in an equal but higher passion. She ministered through the villages and hostels of the city, giving her life in unending ministry where she took little thought of her own health or the common necessities of life. She died at twenty-four years of age, having served two loves in fullest passion. Louis and Elizabeth demonstrate that there is more than a casual connection between human love and the love of God. Both loves are motivated by passions not easily denied. How foolish we are to believe that those who have a great adoration for Christ cease to be sexual creatures. It is tragic that we do not channel our passions and make them usable to God.

Many of Christianity's most noble servants are driven by a passion of the heart that touches hunger and need with new glory. Edward Le Joly wrote of Mother Teresa of Calcutta, "Mother felt intensely that Jesus wanted her to serve him as the poorest of the poor, the uncared for, the slum dwellers, the abandoned, the homeless. Jesus invited her to serve him and follow him in actual poverty, to practice a style of life that would make her similar to the needy in whom he was present, suffered, and loved."[1] In the fervor of this woman's service to mankind, we witness an uncommon ardor that causes her to love with such a passion that every kind of ministry becomes possible.

A second snare laid before the inner life is rarely addressed: gluttony. Food and sex have become the double jeopardy of an affluent Western culture. Restaurateurs and obscenity peddlers continue to keep people occupied with sweetmeats and pornography. Gluttony and libertinism are accepted ways of life. Francis of Assisi felt that his flesh constantly pressed his ego to indulge at the cost of every priority he held.

In the church the dichotomy is blatant. At a recent spiritual life conference I attended, the food brought by the parishioners seemed more central than the spiritual food which the visiting pastor offered from the lectern. At such moments, the word *hunger* becomes so gastric we are embarrassed to call it spiritual.

Gandhi once remarked that those in the abundance of the West were guilty of overfilling themselves. They ate food they did not need just as they devoured other consumer products. No one, he reasoned, would overfill a car with gas, and yet Westerners are surfeited with food.

Hunger is a God-given drive for sustaining life. But gluttony moves ahead of need and eats merely to feel good. Gluttony is a glaring indication of the lack of yieldedness within the Christian community. In banquets and dinners across the nation, we participate in orgies of indulgence. Consider the irony of churches that preach the crucified life while filling their bodies with endless lunches, dinners and brunches.

There are, however, many Christians whose concern about overindulgence has led them to examine anew Christ's command of self-denial. They are looking for practical ways to apply it to their lives. American Mennonites, for example, have published a cookbook containing a call for sensible responses to the problem of overindulging in food. In addition, they exhort us once again to consider the issue of fasting.

Fasting is encouraged in the Bible and has been a part of the church throughout the ages. For generations Catholics taught that communicants should fast before worship. The very idea of *breakfast* suggests by its derivatives that the church promoted the idea of *breaking a fast* only after one had drawn close to Christ in the Eucharist. Protestants followed suit. John Wesley refused to ordain anyone into the Methodist ministry who did not commonly fast. Fasting bears a great witness to our control of our passions rather than our bondage to them.

Power Drive

A third barrier to inwardness is power. Careers, even religious careers, may become forums only for our own advancement. Our longing after Christ must exceed our need for status in the world. The drive for power is common to all. We want to control as vast a domain as possible. Did not the Tempter entice Adam and Eve with the prospect of being like gods? Many assume that Satan incited the primeval pair to lust. Actually, he inflamed them with a lust for power. Satan told Eve she could rise from humanity to godhood in one simple act. In Milton's *Paradise Lost* the Tempter says to Eve, "Goddess humane, reach then, and freely taste."

We may be sure of this: Satan's offer of personal power will always be couched in the interest of God and others. We all like to think of ourselves as generous and self-giving. We all like to hear others tell us how humble or spiritual we are. Such comments separate us from God. Compliments are the parents of egotism and egotism seldom stops celebrating its own power long enough to marvel at God's.

But power, born in church politics and burdensome hierarchies, can also separate us from our Host. James Kavanaugh says he was not able to find God at all while he was a priest. For him, God was born in his very renunciation of the church.

We cannot grasp for personal power and attain meaningful fellowship with God at the same time. Yet this is the heart of religious positivism in America. We belittle Christ by trying to advance both our causes at once. Incredibly, Adam and Eve believed they were actually becoming like God by serving their own interests. When they fled and hid from God the Almighty with their half-eaten fruit, they were ashamed at thinking they were capable of being like God. Their knowledge of good and evil was not a strength.

Religious hucksters still stay too near the tree of good and evil. They advertise their fruit with the promise that our best interest also advances the cause of God. "Make God your copilot," they cry, forgetting that God has his own plans for the destiny of each one of us.

In another day, St. Theresa of Avilà knew that the Host would not join her at the wilderness table if her life was marked by ambition. She begged, in her introduction to *Way of Perfection,* for the church to strip everything from her writing that might embarrass Christ. She pled with Father Presentado to edit or burn her work should it prove only a testament to her ambition.

We, too, must stand against Adam's ambition. We must shun the temptation to become as gods. To linger when we are complimented, to make too much of personal affirmations, to study our own cleverness—all of these can addict us to human praise and steal from us our desire to have more of Christ.

Hurry In, Hurry Out

The last barrier to full intimacy with the Savior is hurriedness. Intimacy may not be rushed. To meet with the Son of God takes time. We have learned all too well the witless art of living fast. We gulp our meals sandwiched between pressing obligations. The table of communion with the inner Christ is not a fast-food franchise. We cannot dash into his presence and choke down inwardness before we hurry to our one o'clock appointment. Inwardness is time-consuming, open only to minds willing to sample spirituality in small bites, savoring each one. It is difficult to teach the unhurried discipline of the table to a culture so used to frozen dinners and condensed novels.

Neither does inwardness rest comfortably with revivalism. It is off limits to those who are in a rush to get to know God. The intense appeals of fast-lane religion are so outward that they miss the heart. Tears and hysteria get in the way of conversation. Fierce emotionalism blinds us to the delights of his table.

Intimacy with Christ comes from entering his presence with inner peace rather than bursting into his presence from the hassles of life. T. S. Eliot well described our dilemma when he wrote, "Where shall the world be found, where will the word resound? Not here, there is not enough silence."[2] The church fathers spoke of *otium sanctum* or "holy leisure." A relaxed contemplation of the indwelling Christ allows for an inner communion impossible to achieve while oppressed by busyness and care.

Perhaps you are wondering how I harmonize what I have said in other places about goal setting and discipline with this imperative for leisure. They are not as contradictory as they appear. When we learn to manage time, we are not managed by time. Once we become masters of our schedule, we will be able to approach God in peace.

Those who have not learned this come to God as they do everything else . . . *late!* They rush into the great white throne, a tornado of hurriedness. They blurt out their confessions and whisk on to the next appointment, glad that they have managed to work God into their blustery schedules.

The *otium sanctum* is true leisure in the middle of a busy life. Most of our hurriedness is really a cover for sloth. When we cram our calendars with appointments, we may delude ourselves that we are busy. But busy about what? We are tending the whirligigs of the trivial afraid that if we stop we will see the emptiness of our lives.

We can hardly enjoy the table in the wilderness if we are always looking at our watches, wondering how much time we may safely give our Host. Holy living is not abrupt living. No one who hurries into the presence of God is content to remain for long. Those who hurry in, hurry out. Holy leisure prepares us to receive the gift of inwardness.

For many years now I have practiced what I call kenotic meditation. The idea first occurred to me in reading Philippians 2:5-8 which states that Jesus "emptied" himself of the glory of God and took on humanity. The word *kenotic* comes from the Greek word meaning "to empty." As Jesus once emptied himself of divine honor to please his Father, so I must empty myself of the hurriedness of life to please Christ.

Before I really begin to talk to God, I like to take a quarter of an hour to shut my mind against the busyness of this world. Incessant chatter fills our thoughts and keeps our brains swimming in images. Joseph Chilton Pearce calls this "roof-brain chatter." We must not only stop obscene or irrelevant thinking. We must deal with the froth and spin of unceasing mental images. This is not easy, but as I move closer to this imageless state of being, my mind slows down to a cleansed level of quietness. At this point, I am able to receive the welcome of the Host with undivided attention.

During my childhood, our house in rural Oklahoma had little furniture on its plain, plank flooring. But if ever we expected company, my mother transformed that little house into a room of grand hospitality. Every visitor was welcomed by a thoroughly clean, neat house. Jesus needs to be shown this same respect.

The emptying of the mind can be achieved with any posture so long as it is in absolute solitude. It is best to close your eyes to eliminate visual distractions. Once your eyes are closed, you simply rest the mind, forcing every thought into silence as it arises. Some have confessed to me that they think immediately of God as soon as they begin the emptying process. But I feel this is unwise. God becomes too quickly wed to images we are trying to clear away. Others have felt that to empty the mind without filling it immediately with Christ will make way for demons. But we are already possessed by the demons of busyness and self-importance.

Louis Evely in *That Man Is You* says there is a hunger for inwardness even in the most derelict of souls because we are created in his image.

> There's something sonly in each human being;
> but how well he hides it,
> and how unskillful we are at finding it!

"In the most heartless miser," wrote Claudel,
"deep within the prostitute and the filthiest drunkard,
there's an immortal soul
which is holily busy breathing
and which,
barred from daylight,
makes nocturnal adoration."[3]

This "something sonly" is the vacuum that strains to be filled until Christ has complete possession.

The young lions roar against our desire to be conformed to his image. Our appetites order us away from the pleasure of our Host. Only as we steel ourselves against their roaring will the table be unspoiled. Then we will sit alone with Christ, ever longing for the life in himself alone. And when, finally, the time comes, our Host senses our love and knows that our hunger for him will bring us back to the table again and again. For the table holds a glory at every phase of life. In his enduring presence, we utter, "Surely goodness and mercy shall follow me all the days of my life" (Ps 23:6).

Why is it that such a simple paradise as he has described never comes?—why is it that these Utopias never arrive upon the map? He answers, because of greed and luxury. Men . . . seldom desire anything unless it belongs to others.

Will Durant

Among the sayings of the Fathers is the story of an important dignitary who gave a basket of gold pieces to a priest in the desert, asking him to disperse it among the brethren. "They have no need of it," replied the priest. The wealthy benefactor insisted and set the basket of coins at the doorway of the Church, asking the priest to tell the brethren, "Whoso hath need, let him take it." No one touched it, or even cared enough to look at it. Edified, and no doubt astonished, the man left with his basket of gold.

Richard J. Foster

The pronouns "my" and "mine" look innocent enough.

A. W. Tozer

3
The Needle's Eye

IN C. S. LEWIS'S *The Great Divorce* a ghost arrives at paradise with a lizard on his lapel. The gatekeeper informs him that lizards are not welcome in the New Eden. He must throw the lizard to the ground and stomp it to death. This will demonstrate that his heart is worthy of the new world. The ghost agonizes over his dilemma. He dearly wants entrance into paradise, but the little lizard has long been his intimate friend. How could he give up his fondest preoccupation? Could he bear the separation? Could heaven be heaven without his dear companion?

What Lewis does not say about the lizard fascinates me most. It has stayed front and center all through the ghost's lifetime, spoiling his appearance, making its demands, soiling his tunic, burdening him with its fatigue, providing him with only a scaly ugliness. But it has lived there with his permission, lending him security. How, indeed, can he give it up without being alone?

The questions are for us as well. If we abandon such dependency, will we find another companion? The man in Lewis's story at last tears the lizard from his clothes and throws it to the ground. Despite its piteous cries for mercy, he crushes it. The corpse of the little beast is then transformed before his eyes. It rises in splendor as a proud steed on which the ghost rides through the gates of heaven in triumph. Out of his poverty and renunciation he rides into a new fellowship with the all-powerful Christ. We cannot arrive at the table clutching our ugly dependence on things other than what our Host offers. Ego is a junk buyer. He hordes old values and ladens us with matchbooks and ticket stubs. He keeps the reminiscences of our most cherished moments and greatest exhilarations, and tells us that this kind of trivia is what matters. He preserves exact records of the times when we found great meaning apart from God. He sifts Gehenna daily for such trinkets as will amuse us.

Too Much Luggage

In the West we have made consumerism a god, and by all the world's standards we are rich. We have all and cannot conceive of abandoning our immense holdings for God. But without a spirit of renunciation we cannot meet the Host at the table.

Self-denial is the only pathway through the needle's eye. "It will be hard for a rich man to enter the kingdom of heaven," Jesus said. "Again I tell you, it is easier for a camel to go through the eye of a needle than for a rich man to enter the kingdom of God" (Mt 19:23-24). The needle's eye is that narrow door to eternal life. We cannot pass through it unless we lay down our cumbersome egoistic baggage. The needle's eye is the only door to Christ's lordship.

We all stumble under the burden of extra luggage. The appetite for having is born in our early years. When my own children were small, they each had their own toy box. They screamed if anyone invaded it. I was making the house payments, providing their food, clothing their bodies. While I provided what they needed, they quarreled over what they didn't need. Well are we called the *children* of God! Even in the midst of his splendor, we crave our small possessions, being all too complacent about what we need the most.

But when is sacrifice reasonable? How much shall we renounce before the flesh is crucified? Such questions are not easy to answer. But if we would know the pleasure of the table, we must deal with renunciation daily. We face the eye of the needle not once, but continually. Each time we are tempted to buy a new home, new car, new clothes, furniture or electronic gadgets, we face anew the issue of two kingdoms: the kingdom of God and the kingdom of this world.

Is it possible to get on well in both kingdoms at once? Jesus warned against a double pursuit saying we could not serve both God and riches (Mt 6:24). The two treasures lie in opposite directions. To move toward ownership in one realm is to disinherit ourselves in the other. I can hear the protests! Don't the wealthy pray? Don't saints own real estate? There may, indeed, be evidences of both. But it isn't easy to find.

Affluent Western Christianity often combines swank Madison Avenue techniques with gaining spirituality through "reasonable" poverty. Low-demand video churches herald the doctrine that God exists merely to meet our needs and whims but not to order our lives. This view often links hands with movements that lead disciples to believe Bible study and limited contributions will make us joyful, diseaseless and rich. No pain is required. No poverty need be endured. Euphoria will come automatically to dispel every barrier to our rosy destiny.

One pyramid-type corporation makes every praying Christian a limited partner and shares the blessings and profits with them. This company bases its whole structure on Matthew 6:33: "Seek first his kingdom and his righteousness and all these *things* shall be yours as well."

We would rather own things than be owned by Christ. We believe we will be respected in this world if we "succeed." But do successful Christians draw people to Christ by their example of success? If so, what sort of Christ are they drawn to? A Christ who enables devout men and women to glory in their substance and never feel guilty for their indulgence?

Thus, in our day, we have pitiful new status-filled disciples —achiever-entrepreneur believers. These "Jesus executives" rule over empires where goods and people are expendable. Thomas Merton once said, "Peace to these is merely the liberty of exploiting others without any reprisals or interruptions." Believe it or not, these double-minded, "successful" Christians may actually affirm how much they hate greed. In reality, they only hate the greed in others.

We try in vain to walk around our own inner urge to get ahead in this world while deepening our spiritual connections. John White has captured our dilemma: "We would like to believe that our treasure was in heaven and that heaven was our real choice. But . . . earthly treasures continue to attract. We may not want outrageous wealth and would be content with reasonable financial security. But we don't want to miss out on anything either. We are ambivalent. . . . We are like the monkey with his fist trapped inside the coconut shell clutching a fistful of peanuts. The monkey wants freedom and peanuts, and he cannot have both."[1] We are spiritually neurotic, trying to embrace indulgence and renunciation at the same time.

Krister Stendahl once observed that no prophet ever had a salary. We fear he is right. Simon the magician once tried to pay Peter to purchase the apostle's spiritual powers. Peter's rebuke was, "Your silver perish with you" (Acts 8:20). Carlyle

Marney paraphrased the passage, "To hell with you and your money!"[2] The words are strong, but they center on the priority of discipleship. God calls us beyond the love of money to the adoration of his Son.

Renunciation Past and Present

We would like to find some way to achieve godliness without repudiating wealth. Many of the best models of true renunciation, dressed in burlap, were called extremists.

Our battle seems set against nature itself. Our appetites are so much a part of us! Not only does it seem fanatical to hunger for inwardness in a consumer world, it marks us as odd and out of step with the values of those around us. We are afraid of being called a prude or a puritan. We are afraid our friends will draw away. Fanatics seem to close themselves in solitude. Prudes and puritans follow a grim Jehovah, gray and severe, who forbids laughter. Howard Hendricks has said, "A Puritan is a person who suffers from an overwhelming dread that somewhere, sometime, somehow, someone may be enjoy himself." We want to live under the proper priorities, but without criticism. We want to renounce without flagging our renunciation in the face of those who would misunderstand it.

Thomas à Becket wore the crown of the state before he wore the mitre of the church. But two facts stand out about the martyred Archbishop of Canterbury. First, he took the part of poor priests against the interests of the wealthy hierarchy. But even more impressive is his close identification with the poor; this was discovered only after his murder. The poor priests who prepared his body for burial found that underneath his regalia he was clad in the simple haircloth of a country monk. The priests celebrated the consecration of the dead archbishop by breaking into joy at worship: "Then the monks wholly transformed with spiritual joy, lifted their hearts and hands to heaven, glorifying God. They gave over sorrow for rejoicing, and turned their laments to cries of gladness."[3]

There are various traditions that surround the conversion of St. Francis. In the Zeffirelli film *Brother Sun, Sister Moon* Francis repudiates his father's wealth in a most unusual way. Standing in the square of Assisi, while the townspeople looked on, he takes off his father's rich robes and turns his naked body to the sunny fields where the lepers and poor lived as outcasts. The townspeople look away in a kind of capitalistic embarrassment as Francis says with determination, "I am born again."

Such a statement about the new birth cannot be equated with the evangelical cliché. Here is the complete and utter renovation of a life and value system. To possess the treasure in the field, St. Francis sold all. He had confronted the needle's eye and won. He banqueted at the wilderness table. But his renunciation had its consequences. Most of those in Assisi thought it a shame for such a talented and wealthy young man to throw his life away.

Imagine that triumphant moment when Thomas à Kempis finished *The Imitation of Christ.* He refused to sign his name to it. For him, it was an offering to the inner Christ. It wasn't so much that he refused to acknowledge the work. Rather, the fullness he knew in Christ dissolved his need for recognition. E. M. Forster once said that whenever our words are truly significant, a signature only detracts from the significance. The ego quickly scratches its gaudy signature over all insignificant art and runs about displaying the piece crying, "Mine. Mine. *Mine!*"

À Kempis had learned a great independence from the demanding, even voracious, appetite for approval. Hearing applause is like drinking seawater; it creates an ever more insatiable thirst for itself. Those addicted to their own popularity often finish life with an alkaline emptiness.

Are there more contemporary examples of renunciation? Only rarely do we see men and women in our day reaching for it. Charlotte Diggs "Lottie" Moon, a Baptist missionary to China, starved to death because she used her salary to feed the Chinese during a famine. Nate Saint gave his life for the spreading of the gospel in this century. These are powerful examples of those who, on every mission field, are performing tireless and thankless service because their treasure is hidden in another world.

Corrie ten Boom, both before and after her concentration camp experience, reached to help all that she could. Before her imprisonment she helped Jews. After the war she worked with refugees and with the mentally retarded. She would take them into her home for whatever ministry they required. She actually initiated a rehabilitation center for war victims in Bloomendaal which still has a ministry to people in need.

Poverty Is Not the Point

In most churches, ministry is limited by socioeconomics. Peter Wagner of Fuller Theological Seminary says that churches grow by adding homogeneous units. This high-sounding blending of the Great Commission with sociology really means that, for the most part, Christianity in the West has not broken free from economic fetters. Thus, it cannot become the kind of church it should be.

But the fault is not uniquely Western. It is a worldwide human frailty. I was once confessing my disenchantment with suburban churchmanship (suburbia is where I live) to a friend who ministers in the Third World. I lamented that some of my members who live in $200,000 homes enjoy more status in the church than those in $100,000 homes. "How I wish I could serve in your country where poverty has reduced all to one common denominator," I told him.

"Not so fast," he admonished me. "In your parish a $200,000 homeowner may look down on a $100,000 homeowner, but in my country families who live in two packing crates look down on those confined to one."

While I was visiting Mexico City some time ago, the comfortable home I stayed in looked over a wretchedly poor section of the city. Their dwellings textured the hillside with slums. One small tarpaper shack rested above a dugout in the hillside. A single, thin electrical wire led into the tarpaper shack. "Do you see that wire?" asked my host. "The family that lives in that shack has electricity. I've watched them for a long time, and I've never seen them speak to the family that lives in the dugout beneath them."

Merely ridding ourselves of possessions is not enough. Renunciation is a matter of the heart. Having is a kind of venom that makes us monsters with status. It takes so little to make us believe we are better than anyone with less. Our Host makes it clear that our emphasis on being must always exceed our emphasis on having.

The gospel does not elevate a mere lack of money. The poor are not to be revered because they are poor. Christ chose to leave heaven not because he despised the riches of glory or adored the poverty of earth. Renunciation was not the point of the Incarnation. His earthly poverty didn't make him Savior and Lord. His willingness to submit himself to the Father did.

Poverty is not the point. Poverty of spirit is. Humbling oneself in obedience to God is positive renunciation. We acknowledge our need, our emptiness, and we are the better for it. Louis Evely confesses that as he grew older, he came to understand the great blessings of poverty. It was not to be avoided but exalted: "We all carry the same burden. . . . Each one groans and sighs beneath a weight that is just a little more than he can carry. He is obliged to acknowledge his poverty. He has need of another. He has need of all the others to help him bear it. The burden that we ourselves bear reveals the burden that is borne by everyone else. Our misery is fraternal; it teaches us about others; it introduces us into the great fraternity of the poor."[4] The poverty of those beneath the cross creates in them a need for Christ. His inner presence becomes for them the only wealth that matters.

How much my understanding grows with the years! When first I received his gift of grace, I thought my best gift to him would be what I owned. During my teen-age years, I shared freely the little wages I received. I had been well taught by my world: money was the great possession; to share it freely was to show great love.

How false my first ideas of renunciation were! My best gift was the gift of myself, given in many years of service to others. It wasn't so much that I had renounced some other pursuit or life-consuming career. Rather, I had such a desire to follow Christ in ministry that I never saw at all the great gift I had been giving. All who have eaten at the table of inwardness have passed by lesser meals. But they never noticed because of their delight in the table.

Spellbound by the Savior

At the Sea of Galilee, Christ called to the disciples to follow him. And so they did, leaving behind their boats and businesses. They were so taken with Christ that they never felt the cost of their renunciation. They walked in the epicenter of a new adoration that had silently slain their old affections. Renunciation that is self-aware is mere asceticism, subtly boasting its own magnificent sacrifice. The apostles came to Christ, having surrendered the possessions that stood between them and the will of God. Even so, we do not remember them because they chose poverty but because they adored Christ. If we too are spellbound by his excellence, relinquishment will be more a by-product of devotion than a prerequisite of it. True lovers of Christ can stand the pain of self-denial. They shine in Gandhi's great truth, "Renounce and enjoy." The glory of the Spirit blinds them to the showy, temporal treasures of earth. They see only the Host. His hands are bruised and scarred; his once-broken fingers now break the loaf.

As his guests, we must turn from a once-selfish life to seek the life of another. The Host had no ambition but to do the Father's bidding. He could not fail at life, therefore, because life held nothing for himself. So our lives must be lived in imitation of our Host. In Gethsemane Christ struggled with selfish desire. As guests at his table, we must come to our own Gethsemane and there drink the cup of the Father's will.

Philippians 2 is worth long meditation on how Christ emptied himself. Likewise our walk with Christ is to be a continuing cycle of emptying and filling. A bucket will carry water in direct proportion to the degree of its emptiness when it is lowered into the well. If there are rocks in the bucket, it will not be able to bring up as much water. Send an empty bucket down the shaft and the filling will be more complete.

Once Thomas Edward Brown was walking along a beach when he reached down and picked up a seashell. As he put the shell to his ear to hear its version of the sea, he was startled as the spidery legs of a sand crab reached out of the opening.

When the old mollusk had died, the crab moved inside the vacant shell. Brown began meditating on the riddle of the indwelling life.

If thou couldst empty all thyself of self,
Like to a shell dishabited,
Then might He find thee on the Ocean shelf,

And say—"This is not dead,"—
And fill thee with Himself instead.

But thou art all replete with very *thou,*
And hast such shrewd activity,
Then, when He comes, He says:—"This is enow
Unto itself—'Twere better let it be:
It is so small and full, there is no room for Me."[5]

We need to pass through the needle's eye and find our place at the lonely table. Our self-denial must become our way of life. Let it not be a showy sacrifice or a boisterous brag, but a quiet turning from our own concern. In self-rebuke, let us listen to the Lord of the Apocalypse: "You say, I am rich, I have prospered, and I need nothing; not knowing that you are wretched, pitiable, poor, blind, and naked. Therefore I counsel you to buy from me gold refined by fire, that you may be rich, and white garments to clothe you and to keep the shame of your nakedness from being seen, and salve to anoint your eyes, that you may see" (Rev 3:17-18).

After Christ said it was easier for a camel to pass through the eye of a needle than for a rich man to enter heaven, the apostles asked, "Who then can be saved?" Their astonishment is appropriate. By keeping the laws, even by giving all to the poor, one cannot be saved. "With men this is impossible, but with God all things are possible" (Mt 19:25-26). We cannot save ourselves by our own renunciation. But as the Spirit of Christ works in us, his handiwork is manifest.

And when all things take their proper place, the towering Christ of the Apocalypse presents himself as our intimate friend. We are alone at the table, and he smiles across as if to say, "I have brought you through the needle's eye. And since you have been faithful over a few things, I will make you ruler over many."

The proudest heart that ever beat
Hath been subdued in me;
The wildest will that ever rose
To scorn Thy cause and aid Thy foes
Is quell'd my Lord, by Thee.
William Hone

Why did the Father give all things into His hands? Because Jesus Christ was completely Man. And He was completely Man because He was completely available! For the first time since Adam fell into sin, there was on earth a Man as God intended man to be!
Major W. Ian Thomas

Look to the living One for life. Look to Jesus for all you need between the gate of hell and the gate of heaven.
C. H. Spurgeon

4
The Christ of the Table

BIRTH IS A DRAMA in which the spotlights fall only on the simple cast of two. In her aloneness, the mother bears down to the blue-white edge of her existence. There, in the dark behind clenched eyelids, is an impatient longing crying out to become. Suddenly, inner life splits forth, and in brilliance cuts to the wholeness of two. And the anguish dissolves into joy at the sound of an infant's voice.

If we could, we would recall the heaving of the natural world that shoved us into independent breath. The warm softness that enveloped our waiting was gone. Dark and heavy circumstance folded in on us, moving us almost against our will. The strictures of the inverted journey were a vise of strangling and painful closeness. (We became compressed, shoved, contorted. We were finally forced forward and lifeward.) All the while, there was in the dark process a golden glory waiting for the anguish to die. Then light spilt across our unfocused souls and we were free, free, *free*!

The process of natural birth focuses the power of Jesus' metaphor. Indeed, we must be born again (Jn 3:7)! In the pain of spiritual birth we are reluctant to venture into new life. We are pressed by the overwhelming dread of our sin. But the time of birth has come. We move along a strange path we barely understand, for we have never traveled it before. The heavy walls of self-doubt and inner confusion constrict in strangling closeness. Why, why, why, God? Why this pain? Why the black mirror of repentance that makes us see ourselves as we are? We cry in the unsure, unfocused, crushing void. Yet it is a warm darkness that aches for the anguish to die. There is a washing of inner light. The long umbilical that bound us to the black is cut, and we are *born again*!

And what is this golden glory? It is the moment of birth and the end of waiting. Living leaps to a bright new focus. All are gone from the drama except the giver of life and the grateful receiver.

Now we look at Christ. For the first time we see the one who labored to bring us to life. He has awaited our coming in steadfast love, and we, so long ignorant of his great love for us, glory in his overwhelming power. We are drawn to him as a child who longs for his parents.

Christ Like Us

Who then is this Christ, this giver of new life, our Host? First, he is like us. Shall we begin this look at Christ with his humanity? As a human, Christ taught us about God as he revealed our own human need. Because Christ was both God and man, we found God understandable. Sergei Kourdakov, a persecutor of Christians, wrote, "The words [of Christ] grabbed my heart. I was somehow frightened and uneasy, like a man walking on unfamiliar ground. . . . Something deep within me, some tiny ember of humanity was still alive somewhere inside me."[1]

Sergei became a Christian because he was touched by Christ, the man who led him, at last, to know the divine Savior.

Our hymns often celebrate Christ's humanness. "What a friend we have in Jesus." "I've found a friend, O such a friend." "Put your hand in the hand of the man from Galilee." "Man of sorrows, what a name." We are drawn to Jesus because he is down-to-earth. He is one of us. Being fully human, he stirs the human within us.

At the table we see the human Christ even as our awareness of his godhood grows. He is truly our "personal" Savior. We meet together as friends. He is not ashamed of his humanity or ours. Indeed his humanity becomes the bridge between his Father and ourselves. His godlikeness redeems, but his man-likeness makes heaven and earth friends.

At the table God is not lofty and throne-bound on a glittering dais. All pageantry fades. How can we help but love the Son of God who stooped to identify with us without resenting our nature? Dorothy Sayers said it well, "He can exact nothing from man that He has not exacted from Himself. He has Himself gone through the whole of human experience, from the trivial irritations of family life and the cramping restrictions of hard work and lack of money to the worst horrors of pain and humiliation, defeat, despair, and death. When He was a man, He played the man . . . and thought it well worthwhile."[2]

God might have been an egotist with no regard for lower life forms. But the world was his second love (Jn 3:16). The great Jehovah, secure in the heavens, without a trace of arrogance stepped into Bethlehem. In that one long step down, humanity took a long step up, and godhood and manhood embraced.

We never can meet him at the table in the wilderness without rejoicing over our common identity. We, through his marvelous new birth, have come to a glorious human life. I marvel at his great love in wanting to be one with us!

Christ Reveals the Real

The Christ of the table is, of course, much more than a mere man. Jesus is the revealer of a reality that is so real it cannot be seen or touched or heard. Beholding him as one of us, we are gripped by the mystery of all that lies beyond us.

This physical world can be magnificent and enchanting. It can and does loudly herald the Creator. Jesus is our great bridge to another reality. Earth *was* his and heaven *is* his. With him, I know that angels are as real as the air I breathe. I am set free from one-story thinking. I am free from the limits of my material self. I can belong to two worlds. I am a citizen in an exciting kingdom "where neither moth nor rust consumes and where thieves do not break in and steal" (Mt 6:20). Christ liberates me from bondage to the individual moments that mortar my brief years together. I can live forever. I surpass time.

Time is a glutton. It chokes down the years. The entire universe is forced to hurry into death. We protest. As Dylan Thomas urged, we "rage, rage against the dying of the light!" But sooner or later, we are gone. Our lives are "swifter than a weaver's shuttle" (Job 7:6). As Shakespeare said, life is a poor player that struts his hour upon the stage and is gone.[3]

Yet for all our protests, there is never enough time. The whole creation is subject to the tyrant of time. Virginia Stem Owens explains the extent of its tyranny.

> The heart of a shrew, like that of many small, furry animals, beats up to 800 times a minute. Such creatures experience more in an hour than we do in a day. They would laugh at our idea of what constitutes flying time. For them the present is a smaller portion, a hundredth of a second; a day is like a year. Their whole lifetime passes in a matter of months. If time runs out so much faster for small mammals than for us, think of fruitflies measuring their generations

> in days. Or exotic elements produced in cyclotrons whose existence is measured in thousandths of a second.[4]

As the Savior calls us to the reality of a more permanent world, he frees us from time with promise: "Whosoever lives and believes in me shall never die" (Jn 11:26).

John Woolman said that this world's goods cloud our vision of the other world.[5] During his life, Jesus constantly denied himself and preached that those who did not deny themselves could not be his disciples (Lk 9:23). The wilderness table is a meeting of two who hold a common denial. The Savior denied himself and finished his pilgrimage two thousand years ago. Only those who have died to self can behold the reality of the next world. Helen Keller once remarked that the things that cannot be seen or felt are the real things. All else is transient. Alive in God, we know the glorious reality we never could have known otherwise.

Christ Completes Us

In his completeness the Christ of the table reminds us of our own unfinished selves. We are in the process of being conformed to the image of Christ (Rom 12:2), but we are clearly not yet finished. In the perfect presence of him who knew no sin (2 Cor 5:21), we behold our imperfection. We move with hope into his presence, seeking his comforting touch.

Our marvelous Christ fosters a yearning in us to become. He doesn't do this by preaching at us to be better. He doesn't beat us down with pain and sorrow so we will become humbled, whipped spirits. Rather he gives us the hunger to become more like himself. Indeed, this is our destiny, for when we see him in eternity "we shall be like him" (1 Jn 3:2).

We are the "not-yet beings." We will never be satisfied until completed. As he once created us physically, he recreates us in the circumstances of life. But we can be confident that "the sufferings of this present time are not worth comparing with the glory that is to be revealed to us" (Rom 8:18).

'Tis the Master who holds the mallet,
  And day by day
He is chipping whatever environs
  The form away;
Which, under His skillful cutting,
  He means shall be
Wrought silently out to beauty
  Of such degree
Of faultless and full perfection,
  That angel eyes
Shall look on the finished labor
  With new surprise,
That even His boundless patience
  Could grave His own
Features upon such fractured
  And stubborn stones.[6]

By whatever means, he deals with the not-yet-ness of our lives. Paul told the Philippians that he was confident that he who had begun a good work in them would complete it in the day of Jesus Christ (Phil 1:6).

There is a sad impiety in the church. We say, "I'm living a pretty good life!" Such pride comes from a dangerous relativism. We define ourselves by comparing our morality with that of others. At the table we are not so haughty. We are not to be neurotic about our unfinished state, but neither are we to congratulate ourselves in complacency or spiritual arrogance. Rather we are to "hunger and thirst for righteousness" (Mt 5:6).

Going to church, as a whole, does little to nurture that

hunger. We are far more prone to discover the shortcomings of others than of ourselves. We the unfinished are intolerant. We are upset that God doesn't do more to make people like Jesus when he saves them. Actually, we are not so offended that others live lives so unpleasing to Christ, but that they are so unpleasing to us.

Early in my ministry I was discouraged that so many in my congregation were "very unlike Jesus." I grew depressed spiritually because I couldn't find brothers and sisters who fully followed the life of Christ. I even began to condemn myself for not making the Christian life more attractive in my sermons.

I was finally cured when I moved closer to Christ myself. It did not improve the general spiritual condition of those around me. But it did help my own poor spirituality and it cured me of self-righteousness.

Coming alone to the table again and again, I found in Christ a readiness to accept me. I was humbled. I was loved in my unfinished state, and found a new graciousness toward others who also awaited completion.

I particularly had trouble with a close friend who loved to have lunch with me. Tom and I always spoke together of our obligation to the cross. But no matter how much we spoke of the love of Christ, he never seemed to be around when the check was delivered. I know it was a small thing, but my irritation grew each time I bought his meal. "God," I prayed, "help Tom see there is a rich testimony to Christ in paying his own way." My heart began to grow as closed toward him as his wallet was toward me.

Only at the table in the wilderness did I begin to see how frequently I had drawn from the riches of Christ and repaid him with a stingy obedience. Tom still isn't very generous, but at least I can pay with greater cheer. At the table I have learned he and I are both unfinished.

Christ's Sufficiency

I have also learned his sufficiency at the table. The glory of all my shortcomings is that God is able to make up the difference between what I need and what I have. "My God will supply every need of yours according to his riches" (Phil 4:19). I have no need to be anxious since God is a sparrow lover. "Not one [sparrow] will fall to the ground without your Father's will" (Mt 10:29). "Your heavenly Father feeds [the birds]. . . . If God so clothes the grass of the field, which today is alive and tomorrow is thrown into the oven, will he not much more clothe you, O men of little faith?" (Mt 6:26, 30).

His sufficiency in the material world is fully matched in other realms. When my infant son was taken with pneumonia, I saw him lying in a makeshift oxygen tent. I was afraid. Monstrously, fear grew larger and larger until it camped like a circle of demons between me and the living Christ. It nearly erased the face of my living Host. Mercifully, his word came to me in power, and I yielded up my fear. "When I am afraid, I put my trust in thee" (Ps 56:3). His sufficiency taught me to trust. My son recovered.

I find that all-surpassing sufficiency that Giles Fletcher spoke of:

He is a path, if any be misled,
He is a robe, if any naked be,
If any chance to hunger, He is bread,
If any be a bondman, He is free,
If any be but weak, how strong is He,
To dead men life He is, to sick men health,
To blind men sight, and to the needy wealth,
A pleasure without loss, a treasure without stealth.[7]

Christ's sufficiency can only be discovered by those who doubt their own ability. Driven before that weakness, they at last arrive and beg for his strength.

Christ and the Father

We learn so much about our Host at the wilderness table. We learn about his compassion. While he cares for all, through the mystery of grace, at the table his entire love and power are focused on us, one at a time. We learn about his dependability. No matter when we flee to the table, we may be sure he is always there. It is we who hurry from his presence, not vice versa. He will never leave us nor forsake us (Heb 13:5).

But greatest of all, we learn about his unswerving and unbroken relationship with his Father. At the table we see that he and the Father are one. They cannot be separated. In the same way we are bonded to Christ. His trust in the Father is a model of how we are to trust him. Even the hell of Golgotha could not break his loyalty to his Father. Just as he never walked alone, so he never comes to the table alone. He brings his Father to the table with him.

Now we know the secret of strength. We too have an enduring relationship. We too have a Father. We are not orphans in this universe. The Father of our Christ is our Father too, and he walks with us though hell should break around us.

This glory is ours: he who meets us at the table will walk with us in life.

Everything leads to union with him; everything brings about perfection excepting sin and what is not our duty.
Jean-Pierre de Caussade

If I dare use the expression, I should choose to call this state the bosom of God, for the inexpressible sweetness which I taste and experience there.
Brother Lawrence

And one has but to note the smug smile of superiority on the face of the one-prayer Christian to sense that there is a lot of pride behind the smile. While other Christians wrestle with God in an agony of intercession they sit back in humble pride waiting it out. They do not pray because they have already prayed. The devil has no fear of such Christians. He has already won over them, and his technique has been false logic.
A. W. Tozer

5
Prayer, the Communion of the Table

THE TABLE IN THE WILDERNESS contains but one loaf. As there is one Lord, one faith, one baptism, so the bread of the table is one communion. But the oneness is born of two hungers: we hunger for Christ; Christ longs for us. The church may create a desire for his fellowship, but its very rituals, public and busy as they are, may obscure the glorious table. Churchmanship alone will never sate our hunger for moments alone with the Host. The joy of our longing hearts not only finds, but desires to remain at the table.

To achieve this oneness is to know true piety: "The key to true piety is not to subscribe to the ethical teachings of Moses or of Jesus, nor is it to have the right precepts of God and reality. Instead it is being united with Christ by faith, then living the kind of life that proceeds from that union."[1] We are not to fear this intimacy, for the union comes as a product of the cross itself. Nothing except our reluctance prevents us from enjoying the intimacy of this union. The middle wall of separation has been broken down and we are free to seek our fill of God's presence (Eph 2:14).

Protestants have often left talk of union with Christ to Catholic mystics. Perhaps pursuing this union does not seem a worthy goal to those missionaries and evangelists. It does not produce "souls at the altar" or provide a framework on which we may hang the ambitious programs of the church or denomination. Some may actually be suspicious of a oneness with Christ so absorbing that people fail to keep the congregational machinery whirring. Machines do not make a kingdom. A king does. At the center of true Christianity lies communion with that King. This communion, whatever we call it, is simply prayer.

Prayer itself is not hard, but the will to pray is. We choose to have other kinds of conversations, so many in fact that we scarcely have a moment of silence. A pastor of my acquaintance puts it honestly:

I find it easier to *preach* on prayer than to *pray*.

I find it easier to *write* on prayer than to *pray*.

I find it easier to *talk* about Jesus than to *pray*.

I find *anything* I do in my Christian life easier than *praying*![2]

Unfortunately, when we talk about prayer we leave the impression that we are people of prayer. But talking about prayer is only talking about conversation. We are not people of prayer until we pray.

Intercession: Make Your Requests Known

For most of us, intercession is the most common type of prayer. We ask God to meet needs. In Luke 18:1-8 Jesus tells the parable of a widow who persistently asks a judge to hear her case and give her justice. Jesus concludes that if an unrighteous judge will answer relentless requests, how much more will God respond to his people? From this we learn first that we can come to God confidently. "Let us then with confidence draw near to the throne of grace, that we may receive mercy and find grace to help in time of need" (Heb 4:16). The widow was not arrogant. She was simply persistent. She believed the judge could be depended on to help. And she would not let go of that confidence. But just as important as his willingness to help was the judge's ability to help. The widow believed in both. If our prayers lack confidence, it may be because we think that God is too small to handle the immense petition we bring to him, or he is not really concerned.

Some teach that prayer is the key to receiving anything we want. We only need "to name it and claim it by faith." If we are sick or poor it is only because we have not prayed in faith. Such Christians quote Matthew 18:19, "If two of you agree on earth about anything they ask, it will be done for them by my Father in heaven," or Matthew 21:22, "Whatever you ask in prayer, you will receive, if you have faith."

The idea that prayer ought to accomplish specific results seems to be overwhelmingly prevalent among Christians in the West. This would certainly seem to be the kind of petition that the importunate widow uses to have her way with the reluctant judge. But let us be honest about the parable. Do judges always answer persistent widows? Does persistent intercession always change things in our behalf? Is it always true that we "reap, if we do not lose heart" (Gal 6:9)? Well has Paul Billheimer asked:

> But HOW can the apparent failures be explained? A few are healed but the multitudes are not. A few have miraculous answers to prayer for healing and prosperity, but most do not. Are all those in this category to give up and wallow in self-pity and defeat? Is one to conclude that the multitudes who are not healed or delivered from grinding poverty must settle for second-class citizenship in the kingdom? Must the

> one who is not healed suffer with a sense of spiritual inferiority and the disappointing suspicion that we can have only God's second best while a select minority who are healed and blessed with affluence pass as "God's chosen few"?
>
> Or is it possible for the great majority who remain financially limited or physically afflicted to make as great a contribution to the kingdom and bring as much joy to the heart of God and win as great an eternal reward as those who are favored with supernatural deliverance here and now?[3]

And worst of all, might not the "answer" obscure God rather than illuminate him? Do we not love the answer rather than the Answerer?

The danger of intercession is selfishness. Crisis intercession is usually offered from deep self-interest. When we are frightened by death or duress, all of our best attempts to focus on the adequacy of God run aground. Many times during World War 2 when Helmut Thielicke was in the shelters, he heard people from his congregation praying, "Lord, save us from the bombs." But their focus was on the attack and not on God. As they prayed, they did not picture God. They mentally imagined bombs hurtling down upon them.

Ego also becomes a bully in such intercession, making strong demands of God. We become like the little boy who just *after* his geography test prayed earnestly, "Dear God, please let St. Louis be the capital of Missouri." The prayer is earnest, but the ego is declaring its own desperate need to be right and challenging God to drop his agenda for the world and embrace ours.

I recently read of a Christian college professor whose baby was very sick. Several times the professor and his wife called in their friends to intercede for the child. The crisis intercession aimed at restoring the child's health, but in a little while the infant died. The zealous professor and his friends continued in prayer, no longer for healing but for the resurrection of the baby. After three days, when the baby had not yet come alive, the local authorities interrupted the prayer meeting and removed the dead child from the midst of the pitiful, grieving parents. The sorrowing couple were doing nothing more than "naming and claiming" what they desperately wanted for themselves.

Praying for ourselves often puts God in a box and makes him the captive of our narrow will and piety. His overall plan, I believe, is not subject to alteration by our will, however earnestly we pray.

What shall we say then? Is intercession wrong altogether?

I do not believe it is, but intercession must always end with the last line of Christ's great prayer in Gethsemane. It was normal and natural for him to ask for deliverance from the cross, but the final decision wasn't dependent on his own desire. The Father had, in the life of his Son, a great plan for redeeming the world through the meeting of their two wills. When those wills met, any petition might have been asked. But the submission of the Son's desires to the Father's plan was evidence of their oneness.

Read John 17 to see how Christ's union with his Father at Gethsemane issued in great prayers of intercession for his church. This kind of prayer is much more rare than crisis intercession. Instead of asking for material needs we ask for truth or grace. Mother Teresa offers us an illustration: "Father, I pray for these sisters whom you have chosen to serve you and belong to you; they are yours, and you gave them to me; you want me to lead them to you; you wish them to be an image of your son, your own perfect image that men might believe that you have sent Him; that seeing their works, men may acknowledge that Christ was sent by you."[4] Constantly she prayed that Christ would be formed in those she served and ministered to.

As Paul wrote to the Galatians, "My little children, . . . I am again in travail until Christ be formed in you" (Gal 4:19). What is this glorious request based on? The desire for our own conformity to Christ.

Here, then, is the threefold secret of intercession. First, we should feel complete freedom to ask a loving Father for the desires of our heart. Second, we must agree that what we want can be set aside to meet the demands of a higher will. Third, our ultimate motivation for prayer should not be that we want something from God but that we want God. As Gandhi wrote, "Prayer is not asking. It is a longing of the soul. It is daily admission of one's weakness. . . . It is better in prayer to have a heart without words than words without a heart. . . . Prayer is the key of the morning and the bolt of the evening."[5]

Let me conclude this section with a note on the glory of honest, conversational intercession. The strength of this kind of prayer is spontaneity. In his journal, John Wesley tells ecstatically of the time he first began to pray extemporaneously. As a high churchman, he had traditionally used liturgical forms. He was so taken with the joy of spontaneous communication that he pledged never to pray rote prayers again. The mystics often used structured communication when they approached Christ, but rote prayers, having been learned by heart, can cease to be a stimulus to the imagination.

Imagination must constantly run on a new track or it becomes lifeless. A living imagination is essential to prayer. When we close our eyes to shut out the near world the images of an unseen world emerge. My own imagination ever sees new visualizations of God, high and lifted up, stooping to my needs, giving me the Christ for whom I hunger. Like Wesley, I rarely pray rote prayers. While it may not be to my credit, I do not actually know very many of them. I find Christ new in every prayer relationship. When the words and images are new, the possibilities and the hope are also new.

Conversational intercession may approach the Father to ask for things. Christ, deeply in love with us, may say no. Whatever his answer, we yet love him because he is Christ and not because he grants our petitions.

Praying for Spiritual Intimacy

Let us now turn to the pursuit of spiritual unity with God. Our basic failure to pray for this intimacy is the direct result of our relationship with him. It is not because we don't love prayer, but because we do not love Christ.

"Oh," we exclaim, "if we'd lived in His day,
if we could've heard
and seen
and touched Him,
how dearly we'd have loved Him,
how gladly we'd have left everything to follow Him!"

Really?
Haven't we ever seen or touched Him?
We can commune with Him every day.[6]

A devoted husband doesn't say, "I love talking to my wife." He says, "I love my wife." St. Theresa confessed that when she first joined the Carmelites, she prayed that God would make her pray for hours every day, as though much rigorous prayer was the quintessence of devotion. God gave her no such schedule. What he did was give her an appetite for himself, and once her hunger for God was whetted, she prayed without ceasing. God does not order hungry birds to eat nor thirsty beasts to drink. Hunger itself seeks food as thirst seeks water.

Alone with our Host, we find the delight of the interior

castle of St. Theresa and the "spouse" of St. John of the Cross. We will pursue our love through a joyous, inner intimacy. In the power of that union we will constantly walk with him in joy.

Near the end of his life, Brother Lawrence reminded us that this gracious, delightful and continuing joy is not always derived from formal worship.

> It is not necessary for being with God to be always at church. We may make an oratory of our heart wherein to retire from time to time to converse with Him in meekness, humility, and love. Every one is capable of such familiar conversation with God, some more, some less. He knows what we can do. Let us begin, then. Perhaps He expects but one generous resolution on our part. Have courage. We have but little time to live; you are near sixty-four, and I am almost eighty. Let us live and die with God. Sufferings will be sweet and pleasant to us while we are with Him; and the greatest pleasures will be, without Him, a cruel punishment to us. May He be blessed for all. Amen.[7]

Brother Lawrence found the blessing of constant companionship with the Son of God. We do not achieve a blending of our spirit with God in some chummy relationship. Rather, we participate in his greatness.

Some kneel and cry out. They weep and laugh hysterically, believing that God is playing across the emotional strings of their nervous systems. When God moves in fullness into our lives, the riches of his glory certainly can be expected to waken our emotional responses. But the key is not the emotional evidence of his indwelling but the indwelling itself. Large evangelistic rallies are often fueled with emotionalism. When sexual intimacy is opened to a group, it at once becomes obscene. Mass spiritual ecstasy can have a similar obscenity.

The intimacy of the table is the glory of our union with

Christ. Believers lost in his company are unaware of the storms of grace they are experiencing. The danger of praying in large groups is a substitution of emotion for union.

Yet we often tremble before the union wrought by the coming of the Spirit. Intimacy with the Godhead terrifies us. But the silence of the wilderness absorbs our fear, and we are enveloped in oneness.

Listening Prayer

Communication is two-way. God's words are fully half of prayer. Buddhists have a koan which asks, "What is the sound of one hand clapping?" We might ask, "What is communication with only one voice?" God is not just an ear but also a voice. If he never speaks, is it safe to assume that he ever listens? A mute God is soon absent. The listening prayer is a prayer of relationship. It is listening silence, shouting silence, but silence nonetheless.

Focus is the major problem in listening prayer. The mind is a busy thoroughfare bearing all kinds of vehicles, each honking to make headway. Earlier I spoke about the emptying process, kenotic meditation. This stops the chatter so we can converse with God in the silence. It cannot be done in a few minutes a day. It occupies a life. Here our humanity becomes more human. Here the image of God in us becomes a clearer mirror of the Spirit. To use Paul Tillich's phrase, our being is united with the ground of all being.

In listening, our inner contradictions are resolved. Our tangled psychology is unraveled.

> What a chimera then is man! What a novelty! What a monster, what a chaos, what a contradiction, what a prodigy! Judge of all things, imbecile worm of the earth; depository of truth, a sink of uncertainty and error; the pride and refuse of the universe! Who will unravel this tangle? . . .

> Know then, proud man, what a paradox you are to yourself. Humble yourself, weak reason; be silent, foolish nature; learn that man infinitely transcends man, and learn from your Master your true condition, of which you are ignorant. Hear God.[8]

Hearing God in our devotion keeps him from being a mute deity. Frank Laubach once saw an enormous dam, complete with turbines and electrical gear. But not a single light bulb was being lit. When he asked why the turbines weren't rotating, he was told the valve was closed. The Almighty wants us to be open to him. Our silence is a door for him to enter.

Madame Guyon once thought that liturgical praying was enough for her spiritual life. Soon she realized that prayer was a conversation between two. Only then did real union occur.

> Oh, my God, if the value of prayer were but known, the great advantage which accrues to the soul from conversing with Thee, and what consequence it is of to salvation, everyone would be assiduous in it. It is a stronghold into which the enemy cannot enter. He may attack it, besiege it, make a noise about its walls; but while we are faithful and hold our station, he cannot hurt us. . . .
>
> The only way to Heaven is prayer; a prayer of the heart, which every one is capable of, and not of reasonings which are the fruits of study, or exercise of the imagination, which, in filling the mind with wandering objects, rarely settle it; instead of warming the heart with love to God, they leave it cold and languishing. Let the poor come, let the ignorant and carnal come; let the children without reason or knowledge come, let the dull or hard hearts which can retain nothing come to the practice of prayer and they shall become wise.[9]

God has, in many ways, taught me to listen in prayer. Once when I put my mind in silence before him I received the clear name of a family I planned to make a pastoral visit to that very evening. I heard nothing audible, saw nothing visual. But a word, an impression, an inner image was born in the silence.

The wife in this family was a Spanish woman who had been in America too briefly to speak English. She was married to an American who spoke Spanish too little to translate effectively. Yet while I readied myself to go to this house, this sensitive man was also at prayer. In the inner conversation of his heart, he received the impression that I was soon to visit their home. The result was that his Spanish wife came to the inner knowledge of Jesus Christ that very night. I have wondered so often since that day how many distinct messages from God I have missed because I was too busy talking to God to listen to him.

Throughout the Scriptures one phrase is repeated hundreds of times, "The Lord said." It is amazing that we are not utterly jolted to a standstill by its frequency! The Lord speaks and they who serve him listen. The Bible itself issues out of the reality of the God who speaks.

All of us have known times when it seemed as though God were not listening. The exact opposite is true.

The more urgent our intercession, the more raucous our necessity roars and leaves God seemingly mute. Grief can roar at such a pitch that God seems silent. But he is not. Like any loving parent, he reaches to his children when they hurt. But hurting children are often too involved in their pain to see beyond it.

Once I saw a child who was playing in the pathway of a huge door at a hotel. Someone quickly entered and threw the door abruptly open. The brass handle of the door struck the child's face. He sprawled backward, covered with blood. Wailing in terror, he ran to his father who tried to calm him down. But the child continued to scream. The child's terror could only be silenced when he was held at arm's length and shaken. The apparently brutal action by one who loved him stopped his loud cries. Then, in the silence of muffled sobs, the child became aware that his father was not only there, but speaking.

Intercession marked by need circumvents what it seeks to establish: an audience with God. Like people who are drowning, our cries for help prevent us from hearing the one who will save us. I am intrigued by the truth of these raucous and doggerel lines:

We mutter and sputter
We fume and we spurt.
We mumble and grumble;
Our feelings get hurt.
We can't understand things.
Our vision grows dim,
When all that we need
Is a moment with him.[10]

A dear woman in our congregation was diagnosed with terminal cancer and began praying for God to save her. She was earnest and in great need. God was reaching to her, but the cancer shouted so loudly she could not see or hear him. In the weeks just before her death, we focused less and less on the crisis. We began to meet for Scripture reading and the prayer of listening. God did not choose to heal her, but we did discover that God was listening, and like God, she learned to listen too. Her listening did not cure her, but in a real sense it healed her. As the cancer grew, so did her inner peace.

Listening in prayer sanctifies our entire world. Teilhard de Chardin said, "Nothing here below is profane for those who know how to see. On the contrary everything is sacred."[11] Teilhard is right, but Romans 10:17 says that faith comes not by seeing but by hearing. For me it is better to say, "Nothing here in this world is profane for those who know how to hear."

Nature may serve as the best closet of prayer. Under the

broad canopy of sky, we may discover the fortress of God. Here in the overwhelming sanctity of the wide outdoors God speaks loudly. Here he uses all he made like a megaphone. His gracious tones reverberate from stars or rocks or hills or streams.

Yahweh is the Hebrew covenant name for God. It seems to have originated in the idea of the God of storms. Yahweh—the desert wind, alive with the stinging, peppering sand that roared over caravans and shepherds' tents. Yahweh cried unto Job from the whirlwind and said, "Where were you when I laid the foundation of the earth? Tell me, if you have understanding. Who determined its measurements—surely you know! Or who stretched the line upon it? On what were its bases sunk, or who laid the cornerstone, when the morning stars sang together, and all the sons of God shouted for joy?" (Job 38:4-7). Here the Maker speaks in the immensity of that which is made, but only to those who are listening.

Christifying Our World

Once we practice inner silence, there is one more principle to help us learn to listen: "Christifying" the world around us. There is no word which adequately describes how praying believers view the world in which they walk. Christifying is consciously viewing the people and circumstances in our lives with the eyes of Christ. Ordinary events become cosmic when seen this way. Ordinary people explode with meaning as we see their potential salvation and service to the Holy Christ. In Christifying, the whole world will speak to us and shout to us of the reality of God. Francis Thompson said he could not even pick a flower without causing an inner trembling in the distant stars.

I love sitting in an air terminal and looking at those scurrying by—unaware of the Christ who smiles and waits to show them his gracious love. At such moments I see that there is an unknown God (Acts 17:23) who needs declaring but who, even before he is declared, sees and loves and yearns to redeem.

I generally think of Christifying my world as painting the face of the Savior on the anxious, hurried faces about me. I write I.N.R.I. on the most tangled of circumstances. As soon as they are autographed with his name, they yield to meaning and to life. A priest in our town, some years ago, happened on an accident where a wrecked gasoline transport trapped a family in a small car while the engulfing flames burned them alive. The priest Christified the crisis. He knelt by the intense heat, his small dark frame silhouetted against the flames, and prayed.

"What good did it do?" That is not the issue. His prayer Christified the event. It called to mind the nature of true reality. There is a world more real than this where God watches and cares and loves. How did the priest manage this Christifying prayer? I suspect he had learned it in a thousand less urgent situations. He had grown accustomed to seeing Christ in every person and to writing the name of Christ on a thousand other events.

Inwardness is found in prayer, listening prayer, and in Christifying our world.

Each night, we should examine our lives:
Did I talk to God today?
Yes, some, but more than talk, I listened.
Did I see Christ in my world?
Yes, I saw nothing but Christ.

And if these are our answers, we have truly prayed without ceasing. We have in such a life exalted the lonely table, and there we dined on a meal of glory. Our inwardness abounded and spilled over into our joyous, silent world.

Learn to obey. Only he who obeys a rhythm superior to his own is free.
Nikos Kazantzakis

We are now a great distance—not only in practice but even in theory—from the fellowship of universal witness. Millions are merely back-seat Christians, willing to be observers of a performance which the professionals put on, ready to criticize or to applaud, but not willing even to consider the possibility of real participation.
Elton Trueblood

Why, then, are you afraid to take up your cross, which leads to the Kingdom?
In the cross is salvation; in the cross is life, in the cross is strength of mind; in the cross is joy of spirit.
Thomas à Kempis

6
The Art of Obedience

THE SINGLE MOST important word in the New Testament is *Lord*. Yet we use it loosely and inconsistently. Jesus asked, "Why do you call me 'Lord, Lord,' and not do what I tell you?" (Lk 6:46). The issue of every disciple is whether or not he or she shall have a lord or be one.

In the rush to Christ, people often agree readily to certain evangelistic propositions. Unfortunately, conversion begins with a person and not a proposition. Lordship is the real beginning of salvation. St. Paul said lordship is the foundation of our relationship with him. "If you confess with your lips that Jesus is Lord and believe in your heart that God raised him from the dead, you will be saved" (Rom 10:9).

In spite of this, some people say, "I accepted Christ as my Savior at a young age, but I did not accept him as Lord till much later." This curious two-step lordship ignores the fact that the Christ who saves can only do so because of his sovereignty. Being saved by Christ without submitting ourselves to him is like being willing to be rescued from a burning building but not having any confidence in the firefighters. Looking down into the net, craving rescue, we can't jump because we don't trust our saviors. Dietrich Bonhoeffer referred to lordless salvation as cheap grace. W. T. Conner put it together when he said, "I accepted Jesus as my Lord, thereby making it possible for him to be my Savior."

Utter commitment to Christ comes from a principle illustrated in Shakespeare's *The Merchant of Venice*. In the play Portia asks each of her three suitors to select the cask containing her picture. One of the three casks is gold. Across the top are the words, "Whoso chooseth me will gain what many men desire." The second cask is silver and across the top of it is inscribed the phrase, "Whoso chooseth me shall get what he deserves." But Bassanio picks the lead cask with the formidable inscription, "Whoso chooseth me must give and hazard all he hath." Here is both the greatest challenge and the greatest reward. The lordship of Christ always comes beneath the inscription of the lead cask.

In a parable Jesus told, a host prepared a great supper and called guests to the event. Each of them turned down the invitation because of other pressing concerns. One had a new bride and could not be distracted from marital pleasure. Another had to break oxen to the yoke. Another said he must survey a parcel of land. In his disappointment, the host opened the party to others who did not have impressive social credentials. They were willing to put the supper of the great host at the top of their priorities (Lk 14:16-24). Lordship supersedes all else. The parable shows both how Gentiles can become a part of the kingdom of God and how the favored people turned their backs on the Messiah's rightful claim on their lives.

Obedience implies submission! *Submission* is a distasteful word these days. We preach freedom and are threatened by every idea of constraint. But we have misunderstood. Is being a "slave" the end of our liberty or the beginning? In some of his letters, Paul calls himself a *doulos christou,* a slave of Christ.

Some years ago Elisabeth Elliot wrote a book entitled *The Liberty of Obedience.* The title drew me to the book. Liberty is enhanced by deliberate submission. In communion with God's Son, the Spirit moves into us and becomes one with us. Mother Teresa, who holds close identity with the Spirit, spends each day submitted to her Father in heaven. "There is no demand so unreasonable," she says, "that God cannot make it of my life."

One couple I know served Christ in Argentina for thirty-five years. The retirement home where they spent their last years was modest but never desperate. An aura of joy enveloped them for they had been set free from every need to serve themselves. They did not horde the days for some agenda of their own. Their love for their Savior made obedience to him a delight. The more they served him, the greater their hunger to serve him. Yet none I have ever met were so free.

One winter I was leading a student conference in Canada when I met the son of a prestigious physician. He was wearing a heavy and handsome winter coat. Complimenting him, I said, "Nice coat!"

"Thank you," he said. In further discussion I discovered that it had been purchased at a secondhand store for twenty-five cents.

"Why did you buy a secondhand coat?" I asked the son, out of earshot of his famous father. "Your father is rich!"

"Because my father also buys secondhand coats."

I listened long enough to discover that the physician had re-evaluated his whole economic position and had led his sons in the same direction. They honored the lordship of Christ by dressing in other people's castaways. They used the money they might have spent on new clothes to travel to Third World countries to practice medicine. Fettered to a great commitment, a doctor had liberated himself and his sons. Such freedom as they knew is only gained as we break our own will and yield to the Savior.

C. S. Lewis once said that the secret of disciplining children begins in the nursery. "While children are young you must break their will, but not their spirit," he said. The problem of self-will is that it usually wills all the wrong things. Nursery children sometimes crave what is bad. They may want to pick up a live charcoal from the hearth merely because the color is pleasing. We may warn them about this, but warning alone may not be enough to break their unwise desires.

Obedience to Christ is born out of our relationship with him. We want him to be part of all our affairs. When we make Christ our constant companion, we are in a relationship which Brother Lawrence called practicing the presence of God. This may also be what Paul meant when he spoke of praying without ceasing (1 Thess 5:17). We might gain much power in our walk with Christ if we could learn such continual preoccupation!

The highest kind of obedience does not come from always asking, "What will you have me do?" but in the moment-by-moment rehearsal of our love for Christ. My wife and I love each other, and as we live in the enjoyment of our relationship, we continually surrender our wills to each other. We do not continually ask, "What would you like me to do?" Because of our relationship, we know each other's desires, and we do all we can to meet them, often without the exchange of words.

St. Theresa said that the best prayer was the meeting of silences; when God's silence envelops us, though no words pass, the presence itself communicates. It communicates the divine will and leaves our own desire empty and waiting for instruction.

The Foundation Word

Study is crucial for sustaining the practice of the presence of God. It is hard work. We would rather rest or recreate. Study demands concentration. It is a discipline that focuses on the glorious Word of God! This is to be understood in the double sense of the written Word of God and the Incarnate Word of God.

Both are real and are bound in one common life from God. Frederick Buechner has combined the two Words, yet offers them in their unyielding individuality:

> . . . God is poet, say, searching for the right word. Tries Noah, but Noah is a drinking man, and tries Abraham, but Abraham is a little too Mesopotamian with all those wives and whiskers. Tries Moses, but Moses himself is trying too hard; and David too handsome for his own good; Elisha, who sicks the bears on the children. Tries John the Baptist with his locusts and honey, who might almost have worked except for something small but crucial like a sense of the ridiculous or a balanced diet.
>
> Word after word God tries and then finally tries once more to say it right, to get it all into one final Word what he is and what human is and why the suffering of love is precious and how the peace of God is a tiger in the blood.[1]

The written Word reveals the living Word. The written Word must be studied if indeed we would know the living Word. I have dealt with study in *The Taste of Joy.* But here I want to concentrate on how the Bible becomes the foundation of the inner life.

To know the Bible is not an option for those who want to know true inwardness. No one stays at the table long who does not also study Scripture. Mystics without study are only spiritual romantics who want relationship without effort.

The best learning of Scripture is not done in a theology class or in the high towers of religious institutions. The written Word of God came originally from the pens of forty writers over a period of 1400 years. These people were sometimes caught in the snare of historic upheavals. They suffered martyrdom and endured the pressure of imprisonment and the horror of military sieges. They did not write in the peaceful calm of seminary chapels but in the hurriedness of unsure days. Likewise their writings are meant to speak practically in the hurried days of our own lives. If this seems to contradict what I have said before, remember that the congestion of living can also draw us to the instructive silence of the table.

Jesus by-passed the scholarly in favor of the simple. To make his truth both memorable and usable, Jesus worked with what was close at hand: wildflowers, fig trees, mustard seeds, lamps, baskets, shepherds, sheep, weeds and wheat. He never did an exegesis of a Hebrew root or compared the Aramaic and Sanskrit origins of ideas. His truth was, nonetheless, profound. Academicians find meaning the same way as those who will never be scholars.

Even great scientific truths are discovered far from the classroom. Galileo first speculated on the properties of pendulums by watching a swaying chandelier during a boring hour in church. Einstein conceived of relativity while stuck in a station waiting for a tram. As he watched the clock, he wondered what would happen to time and mass if the tram could travel at the same speed as the light in the station that brought the face of the clock to the retina of his eye.

Just so, Scripture reveals truth through everyday occurrences in the lives of the Bible writers. Jeremiah watched a potter working with poor clay and used that to illustrate Israel's stubborn refusal to be molded. Hosea's wife chose lovers, and in his broken heart the prophet saw the unfaithfulness of a nation.

Paul saw a grafted tree and spoke of the new branch of gentile Christianity.

Of course truth can be learned in seminary, but it is not the only place. Otherwise the masses of Christians are denied their God-given right to truth.

God spoke truth in earlier days to the Bible writers. He speaks truth just as loudly today when we study the Bible. However, we must remember, as Jean-Pierre de Caussade wrote, that "we are in an age of faith, the Holy Spirit no longer writes gospels, except in our hearts; saintly souls are the pages, suffering and action the ink. The Holy Spirit is writing a living gospel with the pen of action, which we will only be able to read on the day of glory when, fresh from the presses of life, it will be published."[2]

There is a proverb which says: "I practice daily what I believe; everything else is religious talk." Only God's Word mixed in life can make Scripture serve inwardness. For inwardness can never come at the price of withdrawing from our world.

> Far too many people have used the Bible like a medical student uses a cadaver. They examine it, dissect it, perform surgery on it, familiarize themselves with it, and learn its distinctive qualities. But as that future doctor cannot give life to that dead piece of humanity, so these people never get the Word alive in their life. They somehow fail to remember that the people who hated Jesus most were biblical scholars and had Scriptures over their door posts, strapped to their bodies, and quoted chapters of it when their narrow-minded interpretation supported their warped views.[3]

Scripture used only to fortify theology is quarrelsome. Someone always wants to discuss the "discrepancies" in the Bible. But when reason seems at an end and life is desperate, we do not pick up the Scriptures to search for discrepancies, but truth.

Certainly in our devotion, we should not lose respect for biblical scholarship. We should always try to give reasonable answers to sincere questions. The laboratory of life will not teach us all we need to know. In life Scripture is made practical, but in disciplined study it is correlated in ways that cement it together. Here the mind yields up its stubborn ignorance, so that we come to the wilderness table ready to learn the written Word from the Word made flesh.

The Sign of Inwardness

Jesus often took time to be alone to pray, but these times were always retreats. Between his periodic withdrawals, he touched and healed. He became the hands of God. In ministry, we become the hands of our Host.

Inwardness becomes true substance only when we leave the table to serve in his name. Fénelon called for Christians to maintain a balance between learning and doing. He pointed out that learning rarely makes us want to do—it only breeds the desire for more learning. "We are in danger of evaluating our spiritual maturity on the basis of the knowledge we have acquired."[4] At its great heart, the kingdom of God has great compassion for the world. We are not free to hide anywhere from our responsibility, especially in the bosom of God.

Francis of Assisi is a familiar example of inwardness that did not hide in God but deliberately chose to be the instrument of his peace. The true sign that Christ indwells our lives is that we turn outward to display the same kind of compassion that he did.

A friend who serves a rural parish has large talents though his church is small. Yet there is no hint of resentment that God has passed him by in giving promotions to others less talented and educated than he. He seems not to notice. He has learned inner listening, and his listening life marks him as a man of rich possessions. It is hard to tell whether his active compassion for others taught him inwardness or inwardness taught him to minister. He visits the aged who live and die with few to care for them. He touches the blind and embraces the feeble. Christ reaches through him. As I watched him one day, it seemed that I heard the Savior say, "As you did it to one of the least of these my brethren, you did it to me" (Mt 25:40).

Inwardness cries with the reaching arms of Christ, "O Jerusalem, Jerusalem. . . . How often would I have gathered your children together as a hen gathers her brood under her wings" (Mt 23:37). Certainly there is danger others will take advantage of us. But as Fénelon says, "Happy is the one who pays no attention to his own hasty judgments nor to the gossip of others! . . . You must learn to despise the selfishness of your own heart, and you must also be willing to be despised by others. . . . Learn to draw your strength and nourishment from Jesus, and from Him alone."[5] As we serve, we may be taken for granted, but we must remember Jesus' words, "the Son of man came not to be served but to serve, and to give his life as a ransom for many" (Mt 20:28).

People continually called out for mercy when Christ was occupied with other matters. But he knew that there were times to serve, even if it interrupted his personal agenda. Someone once asked a pastor, "Do you like all the congregational interruptions in your work?" to which he replied, "My work is my interruptions."

Jesus came to be interrupted. This is the nature of a rescue operation—whether it be to the sick, the aged, the mentally ill, the lonely or the spiritually lost. Jesus "came to seek and to save the lost" (Lk 19:10). And these need to become the target of our ministry as they were his. We cannot minister as Christ did unless we can see people one at a time. We must engage in rescue work without falling into the snare of mass promotionalism. It is all too easy to be seduced into using evangelistic sales techniques. Rather we must simply follow the lead of Christ in obedience.

My own spiritual gift seems to be evangelism. Each time I open the New Testament to share Christ, I feel his strong inner approval. This is true whether or not those I talk to ever come to know him. For in the very sharing of the gospel, I know obedience to the final great command of Jesus Christ to go into all the world (Mt 28:19).

On those occasions where I actually lead others to faith in Christ, I find an overwhelming inner joy in the Holy Spirit. I have also had the more enduring joy of seeing those in Christ continue to triumph over the very needs and fears that first made them open to his love.

The Host at the table in the wilderness does not congratulate me. This is why I myself was born anew. He does not think I am better than others with different gifts. We glory together in the certainty that his kingdom is growing. That is a joy for both of us.

Submitting to Sovereignty

Often we mistakenly pursue the deeper life rather than obedience. A Bible expositor once asked his little boy to carry out the trash. His son replied to this command by saying, "Oh, Dad—you are so beautiful—you are the true giver of all things. I think I will just stay here and contemplate your face." These were nice words, but they were not obedience. In fact, without obedience we have reason to doubt the depth of admiration altogether.

Most people live powerlessly today. They prefer to live in indulgence than to know the discipline of the table. They choose ease and complain that they find no deep satisfaction in Christ. Self-will always hungers for the fruits of obedience without the effort of it.

Obedience is first an unfolding of ourselves before our heavenly Father. Christ had no secrets from his Father. He maintained a transparent mind and conscience. So we must seek to make our lives transparent before God. God ever is prying the lids off our closed minds to let in the light of his holiness. We flee this disclosure. Foolishly, like Adam, we try to hide. But God continues to pursue us crying, "Where are you?"

Refusing to be open to him, of course, cannot shut out his scrutiny. But our openness is a willingness to look at ourselves with him. Repentance is not the exposure of our evil hearts but looking inward with God in weeping agreement about our condition. Here in the final end of pride, we wait for him to cleanse us.

Then we are ready for submission to his will. Christ purchased his universal authority by his obedience. His life tells us plainly that the crown of victory is forged from the gold of obedience. Likewise our Christlikeness is gained on the basis of our willingness to do his will. When we voluntarily come under divine command, our lives feel a wideness growing inside until he is there, reigning on the inward throne of our joyous desire to serve him.

After we have opened to God and submitted to him, we begin to yearn for complete identity. How could Christ stand before Pilate in complete self-assurance? The crowd had stripped him of his dignity, yet Christ gloried in his Father. Like Jesus on trial, we gain strength for an ugly moment by a focus on the One who is our identity. We find this identity as we obey him whose lordship is our delight. As Christ served others to please his Father, so we must minister to please Christ.

I once had a friend who suffered from a disease that finally claimed his life. When he was first diagnosed with it, he said, he began to separate the things that were eternal from the things that were less enduring. Like so many pastors, he had devoted most of his life to church administration and congregational concerns. But during this crisis he began moving away from the "things of God," and toward God himself. At last, he experienced a hunger to be like Christ. He no longer prayed for healing but for identity with his Lord.

When Helen Keller was about six years old her aunt made her a doll out of towels. It was a shapeless and improvised thing. But the first thing that Helen noticed when she picked it up was that the head lacked eyes. Not being able to see herself, she insisted that her aunt make the doll better than she was. She tugged at her aunt's string of beads and laid them approximately where the doll's eyes should have been. Her aunt touched her eyes and then the doll's head and Helen nodded yes. The aunt found two buttons and sewed them on. Here is the hunger to be better than we are.

Somehow I know that search.

Jesus is that hunger. We want to be made like him, re-created in a new way to look like Jesus. Like Helen, we tug at better images, crying to be remade, fashioned in an ideal form—like the very Son of the Almighty God.

We are loved by Christ who identified with us by becoming one with us even at the expense of death. In his dying, he was able to love and forgive his executioners because he knew who he was. In his faithful following of the whole will of God, he taught us obedience. Until we obey, the words *Lord, kingdom, study* and *ministry* are dead. But in obedience such words live. And we are filled with more than self.

Obedience is a celebration of two minds bound in one desire. We know a glorious togetherness with Christ: the fellowship at the lonely table is ours. We may come to eat as often as we will, but we must remember this: those who would eat must obey.

The talk was still going on when, quite suddenly, a young violinist appeared on a balcony above the courtyard. There was a hush as, high above us, he struck up the first great D minor chords of Bach's Chaconne. All at once, and with utter certainty, I had found my link with the center.

Werner Heisenberg

Things mean as words mean. We speak words; God speaks things. He opens what we suppose to be his metaphorical mouth, and out tumble trees, viruses, moons.

Virginia Stem Owens

Flower in the crannied wall
I pluck you out of the crannies,
I hold you here, root and all, in my hand,
Little flower—but if I could understand
What you are, root and all, and all in all,
I should know what God and man is.

Alfred Lord Tennyson

7
Widening Our Intimacy with Christ

ONE DOOR OPENS to the world of the spirit: imagination. God's realities start at the threshold of our senses. But they go far beyond sight, smell and sound. That is why we often miss him altogether. To follow Christ we must create in our minds God's unseen world, or never confront it at all. Thus we create in our minds the Christ of the table. It can seem irreverent to take the God of galaxies and fit him in a chair the same size as ours. But size is not the important issue. A clock is not more accurate than a watch just because it is larger. We come to God because he alone gives meaning to our world and not because he is big.

We also imagine God on a grand scale. We think of angels and devils and harps and flames and white thrones and gold-paved cities. Each of us imagines differently. Our inner visions are shaped by the world we live in. In Sunday school, Black children tend to draw Black Saviors and White children, Caucasian Christs. And it is not just the children. Even as grown men and women, we tend to see Christ rather like ourselves.

Still, imagination stands at the front of our relationship with Christ. We cannot commune with a Savior whose form and shape elude us. Whenever I speak long distance to my son or daughter, I use their voices to hang a thousand images of who they are. Likewise, in my conversation with Christ, I see him white robed, yet at ease in my own time. I drink the glory of his hazel eyes, thrill to the golden sunlight dancing on his auburn hair. I see his calloused hands reaching out for me and for all the world he loves.

What? Do you disagree? His hair is black? Eyes brown? Then have it your way. His lordship is your treasure as it is mine. His image must be real to you as to me, even if our images differ. The key to vitality, however, is the image. And where did the image come from? From hundreds of books and paintings. From a thousand sermons and Sunday-school lessons. The image rose from the low altar of repentance and climbed to the high altar of faith.

The Bible's Imagination

Bit by bit, block by imaginary block, we define him and we adore him. The Bible writers did the same. Their definitions did not make God more real, but they did make his vastness more manageable for our minds.

Is it necessary to define God? Is it fair to limit the Almighty so? Oceans can never be known, but a single drop of the Pacific tells us the essence of all. While God's reality remains hidden, he discloses himself to us in finiteness. This is the meaning of Christ becoming a man.

What of those who lived and served him before Bethlehem? Abraham heard the voice, "Go from your country . . . to the land that I will show you" (Gen 12:1). What was the mental image he had of the God who spoke? We cannot know. Yet his image was powerful enough to motivate him, as a very old man, to undertake a perilous journey. Abraham believed God. God was a powerful reality he dared not disobey.

Shall we go on? At a burning bush, Moses encountered the God of Abraham. How strong was his mental image? He went to Egypt and stood against the greatest power in the world with a demand: Let my people go. His courage must convince us—he held in his imagination a God who was sovereign.

The psalmist imagined God as a shepherd (Ps 23), a light (Ps 27:1), a shield and buckler (Ps 18:2), a king of glory (Ps 24:10), and a fortress (Ps 91:2). Isaiah saw him as a great heavenly monarch whose train filled the Temple (Is 6:1). John the Baptist saw him as a harvester (Lk 3:17). Paul as a righteous judge (2 Tim 4:8). Jeremiah as a potter (Jer 18:6). Each of these men in turn served the God whose image motivated their obedience.

Our own devotion to God also comes from the image we hold in our minds. While Job 38:1 uses a violent whirlwind to describe God, we must not consider Job a pantheist. God is not nature. He presides above it.

God can speak to us in such a great variety of ways that we must learn to listen in many ways. Going into Jerusalem on Palm Sunday, Jesus said that if the pilgrims and citizens of Jerusalem had not proclaimed him Messiah, the very rocks would have done so (Lk 19:40). Paul said that the whole creation groaned waiting for its redemption (Rom 8:22). Isaiah even said that in the coming Zion, all of nature would be transformed so that the bear and cow would graze together, and babies would play with snakes (Is 11:7-8). Psalm 96:12 says that all of the trees of the wood rejoice at his coming. Psalm 19:1 says that the heavens declare the glory of God and the firmament shows his handiwork. We must stay alert because God is ever speaking to us.

Where Shall I Go?

But even more than the natural world, God is filling all of life with himself. Jesus said that God is a Spirit, and we must worship him in spirit (Jn 4:24). There is an immense wideness in this statement. God pervades the rocks and rills and hangs about us in the air. Paul reminded the Athenians that in God we live and move and have our being (Acts 17:28). Whether we believe in God or doubt him, we must do it from the center of God, for that is the only place we can live.

I have had many people tell me that they didn't see how they could ever live up to Paul's admonition to pray without ceasing (1 Thess 5:17). But we define prayer by the image of God we hold. If we see God on a great white throne, then we see prayer as a coming and going from his presence. But if we see God as One who infiltrates the very atmosphere around us, then every word we speak will be heard, every action will communicate a message to him. All of life becomes communion, for he fills the very crannies of our minds and bodies. Even our thoughts form before his full awareness.

Our world will change as we widen our view of God. We know who he is, but we also need to understand where he is. God continually accompanies us. So let's not act as though he is somehow "out there" and that we must "go" to talk to him.

Most of us see our relationship with God like a marriage. We get together with God in prayer much as a husband and wife get together at the end of the day. From breakfast to supper, marriage is less "together" than when the spouses are physically in each other's presence.

I have heard Christians say, "We must take time for God." Or, "I get up every morning at six to pray and have fellowship with God." Or, "Between three and four is my throne time!" God does preside from the great throne before the glassy sea (Rev 4:6), and it is good to have special times focused on God.

But he also stretches as far as existence itself. We must not fasten him to some specific place and act as though *only there* we can meet him.

The marvelous Christ pervades the entire world of thought and study. We have nothing to fear therefore by growing in many directions at once. In fact, the more we know of psychology or literature or mathematics or philosophy, the wider our perception of God becomes.

J. B. Phillips, in his well-known book, grieved that our God is too small. If this is true, it is because we give him only the religious space in our lives. As we allow God to be in charge of more of our world, then I believe our understanding of his immensity will grow. But growth can be painful. In some ways I found it easy to be a fundamentalist in Oklahoma in 1950. Now pat answers and rigid categories do not satisfy the hungers of my heart. I was more certain of everything when I first knew Christ. I had read so little and had lived such a short time I had neither books nor experience to blunt a clear understanding of my unstudied world. In widening all I knew of the world I found answers coming slower and my assessment of people and their beliefs and relationships harder to define. But the growing made me less of a know-it-all and more prone to listen to questions, even when I had no certain answers.

No one pays more for their faith than Christians with growing minds. When we place expanding information against the truth of the gospel, we beg for more light. God literally crowds all good books. He inhabits the theater and the laboratory. He is alive in every conversation between those whom he has created. God's glorious, all-pervading self awakens us to his immensity. We may celebrate him wherever we are. He is all about us: the very wallboard of our offices. He is the floor and ceiling, ground and sky. He is below the floor, above the ceiling and beyond the wall. Wherever we walk, we push against him, and yet do not for he swims through us, blessing this his glorious inwardness-outwardness-upwardness-downwardness.

Then where shall we go to escape him? It cannot be done.

O LORD, thou hast searched me and known me!
Thou knowest when I sit down and when I rise up;
  thou discernest my thoughts from afar.
Thou searchest out my path and my lying down,
  and art acquainted with all my ways. . . .
Whither shall I go from thy Spirit?
  Or whither shall I flee from thy presence?
If I ascend to heaven, thou art there!
  If I make my bed in Sheol, thou art there!
If I take the wings of the morning
  and dwell in the uttermost parts of the sea,
even there thy hand shall lead me,
  and thy right hand shall hold me. (Ps 139:1-3, 7-10)

Since he is always with us, let us open the fissures of our being and joyously admit him. Then we will find him leading us, following us, soaring over us and sitting in quietude to hear us, even as he waits on the throne to hear our coming.

Our communion with Christ is measured in two ways: we are ever in him, yet always coming to him. We walk in his wideness, yet we seek him at the table, knowing that his table presence cannot ever be contained in such a little space. The danger of emphasizing only the table is that we might start believing that all other time is wasted. Rather than this, let us widen our definition of intimacy.

The God of the Parade

The God of Psalm 139 is the God of the parade and the marketplace and the wilderness. Let me discuss God in each of these categories.

For years, I met God only at church or in some quiet corner of devotion. How wrong I was! Jesus lived in the streets of his day where he saw his Father in the needy faces of those he met. In the hilarity of the moment, the all-adoring Christ took part in the laughter and the wine. The Christ of the parade was even called a glutton and a drunk (Mt 11:19). At dinner parties he chatted with the beloved sinners because God dwells in the thick of people. Thus, all parades are sanctified.

How can we harmonize the Christ of the good time with Christ the Redeemer? Do parades belong in the lives of Christians? Aren't they set against the spirit of our commitment to Christ? Every parade causes me to see the crowds parting for a young rabbi seated on a donkey. Is there none in the Macy's Parade to cry "Hosanna!"? Very well, then the curbstones will cry out and the pavement itself will shout for joy. Here where the crowd is heavy the Savior still seeks the lost and disconsolate, even in the midst of laughter, bands and clowns.

But those who call upon him for salvation seldom do so at a parade. Here they merely play horns or stuff roses in the floats. Perhaps the parade shows us our worst, celebrating ourselves in the eating of peanuts. Still, God the lover is here and looks out with a better assessment. Remember Christ as he looked down from Olivet upon an ancient parade—a religious festival—and laments, "Would that even today you knew the things that make for peace! But now they are hid from your eyes" (Lk 19:42). The city did not suspect they were observed in their empty merriment by a wistful Savior. The heart of God calls him to love and watch the parades. Never in his eternal history has he missed one.

I went recently to a movie with an edifying theme. I thanked God during the film for the great artists and writers committed to noble themes. I once watched a tense football game. As I viewed the coach in the tightest of moments, I remembered that he was reputed to know Christ. I thanked the Lord for him and for a game where his own concepts of integrity marched across the football field. Did God care who won? No, unlike myself, he had not picked a team to champion. But wherever there are crowds of souls, God will be in the midst of them.

We who contain Christ sanctify the parade. Emily Dickinson wrote:

Much madness is divinest sense
  To a discerning eye.

Once, in a crowded shopping mall, I spied a teen-ager sitting quietly on a rising cascade of stairs. He was alone. His eyes called me. I spoke to him. The sanctifying God had me sit, and as we spoke, our conversation turned to his lonely, heavy heart. It was odd, for while I have often spoken of Christ in such places, the busy mall was suddenly stilled with God's presence as we prayed together. There in the madding throng, the world stopped for his great glory.

The God of the Marketplace

Just as Christ can be found in the parade, we must also allow him in the marketplace. Too often, the Christ of the wilderness table is excluded from commerce and career. We somehow feel that Jesus must not understand the wider world of business. Jesus seems spiritual and the business world seems so unspiritual. Thus we think there are two kinds of Christians: clergy and laity.

We are foolish to have allowed Christ and commerce to become so separate. I have always been energized by new Christians who don't see life this way. They assume Christ is Lord of all. They have not allowed their world to be divided. They take their Savior, in the joy of their new relationship, into offices and shops. Before long vibrant Bible studies and prayer groups spring up around them.

The Christ of the wilderness table sits now in the company cafeteria or the board room. On the faces of fellow executives or in the computer seminars, we see his likeness. Is this great Christ out of place? Hardly. He once interrupted fishermen, and they left a thriving business to follow him. He called Matthew, an internal revenue man. He spoke to politicians like Pilate on the nature of power. He called those who made a living in prostitution to seek love in himself.

This is the radical claim of the Christ who meets us at the table: let me go to work with you! Psychologists and industrialists long ago discovered that much of our meaning in life comes from the hours and years we give to making a living. Therefore, we sin greatly when we make no effort to integrate Christ (who is our ultimate meaning) into our livelihoods. While we would always introduce two good friends to each other, we do, in fact, separate Christ from our career.

Rather we should sanctify office buildings and warehouses and refineries and assembly plants. These are temples too. In these great buildings, God walks among forklifts and is desperately in love with those who wear hard hats or carry steno pads. One person I know became a Christian because someone asked him to pray in a company cafeteria. Jesus' Great Commission can just as well be translated: Since you are going into all the world anyway, why not take the gospel with you? (Mt 28:19).

The God of the Wilderness

More than the parade or the marketplace, I am most intrigued by the Christ of nature. Here the table in the wilderness ceases to be a metaphor and becomes reality. I never love Christ more than when I meet him in a lonely moment in the center of his natural world. Here the Christ of the table shouts his truth. His profound intimacy is a walk in the wilderness when the air is charged with God and he touches us with his own self. The cliffs rise and wild woods sing the song of the morning stars (Job 38:7).

One August I went with my wife for two days to a national monument in New Mexico. We were captivated by the majesty of the place. Rising on either side of our lodge were towering sandstone cliffs where the Anasazi (or Ancient Ones) had once lived. Now their caves were dark and silent. Here and there one could see the enduring evidence of their primeval fires. Still, there was no sound in the valley. The enchantment of the forest was invaded by the Christ. His fuchsia sunset set the gorge ablaze. His incandescence quickened the desert stars.

I awoke before dawn and walked alone at daybreak, high upon a narrow ledge. There I waited for the sun which vaulted up at once above the canyon rim. With stark suddenness, it inflamed the world with fire. "Oh Christ, here is my canticle to the sun—no, no, it is my canticle to the *Son*; let us behold our Father together!"

Here I celebrated with the Christ of the table. I am a new creature in Christ, born again in a love that shall outlast the very sun that flings itself at me. Our love shall endure and I shall stand one million years from now with this my glorious lover. There we shall be one. We shall not behold each other from opposite sides of a sunset, but face to face (1 Cor 13:12).

How lavish is this God? He declares himself far beyond our ability to notice. I was hiking a deserted trail in the Grand Canyon, when God's flair for color exploded in desert anemone all around me.

"Why, God?" I asked him. "No one will see this shouting color. No visitor will pass on these wild, unwalked meadows."

It seemed that God replied, "If I declare myself beyond all human hearing, then let my declaration be for us to celebrate wherever we walk together."

Do we fear a devotionalism that makes us celebrants of nature more than of God? We must not overreact. Even we who adore Christ are part of the very nature which calls us to Christ. René Dubos says it is the vibrating, alluring side of nature which causes us to make a response to the universe as a whole: "Animism persists as an undercurrent in all great religions which, in their highest form, involve the response of the person as a whole to the universe as a whole."[1] What a pity that we do not see the God of the universe as a whole or celebrate him that way in church. We celebrate the God of liturgy or the God of the proposition or the God of theological excellence or the God of religious inspiration. But we by-pass the God who is the universal reason behind all reasons.

We can learn so much about him in the natural world where he is so at home. Here everything is to be sung until all the individual notes resonate with God. Like Siddhartha at his river, I see and feel a God who observes me, yet fills me. He sits with me, yet is Father to Jesus Christ and reaches to make me one with all I behold in the lonely wilderness. Virginia Owens reminds us that "Einstein worked for three decades on his unified field theory, trying to connect gravitational and electrical fields in coherent equations. He is generally considered to have failed in this effort. But he left behind this conceptual possibility—the picture of the universe as a pulsating single organism."[2]

We thank God that we are made and that all that is made is his and is good. His great lessons of harmony sing of our togetherness with his whole created order. Virginia Owens awakens us to God, the cosmic ruler, when she says, "I have stumbled on the tracks of a field mouse embroidered on the snow where they emerged from a tiny tunnel, and have followed them to where they disappeared in a huge feathered fan swept into the snow's surface by a bird's wings. And I have given thanks for the mouse and thanks for the bird and thanks for the tracks they left, like notes, scored on this vast white sheet for the one who spies them out to sing."[3]

I picked up a sego lily once from the desert floor and marveled over Jesus' proclamation, "Consider the lilies; . . . even Solomon in all his glory was not arrayed like one of these" (Mt 6:28-29). I am made and yet I worship by crying out, "O LORD our Lord, how majestic is thy name in all the earth!" (Ps 8:1).

How pitiful if we keep him only as a little devotional guide or doctrinal statement! We had better let God grow! Then in the art galleries of our world we will see him in the colored pinpoints of the impressionists or the heavy umber warmth of Rembrandt.

Were any of these artists atheists? No matter. God exists in the very threads of his canvas and will not be denied. Was the composer an unbeliever? Never mind. His unbelief will not lock God from the concert hall. Is a book a great piece of literature but doesn't concern itself with God? Nonsense. If the book contains any beauty or makes any sense, it has come from God as surely as did Jesus. Not only has it come from God, but God inhabits its very paragraphs, and page by page we will meet the incognito Jehovah who passes truth from the paragraph to our retina until we cannot even consider the page but rejoice in the light.

When I stop my hurrying, then the God within me can hold a lively dialog with the God who is beyond me. How can this be? Within and beyond? I am too small a vessel to contain much of God. Yet I, crowded with his presence, discover that my humanity is but a thin separation for the God I both contain and approach. I am called from the inner alter of adoration by a thousand things that beckon me to see his greatness beyond the narrow borders of my spirit.

I watched a nativity scene at church in which a real infant played the part of the baby Jesus. Suddenly, the baby stretched his hand up through an opening in his blanket and there, silhouetted in the light, was a magnificent declaration. Five perfect, tiny fingers stretching and curling. The hand cried out, "Here is God . . . here . . . Here . . . *Here*!" And the God who made the hand and declared himself in it suddenly welled up in my own life. Saturated in his glory, he and I were enfolded into oneness. I beheld him. Yet I couldn't behold him, for I was one with him and too much a part of him to stand outside him and see him. Somehow lost to myself, I knew what heaven must be. When his presence and mine become fused, I am no more, and yet more than I have ever been.

I know now the great truth of the wilderness table. I will never force the cosmic Christ into some corner where I may feed him sour bits of church life. Nor will we meet only where the institution agrees to our meetings. He will be mine in his own music, and I will be both his song and his enthralled hearer. At the table, we shall talk of our love, and everywhere else we shall glory in it. Thus the intimate wilderness is expanded till all parades and markets and all nature itself yields to his presence and are glad to host his silent, yet roaring reality.

Because I could not stop for Death,
He kindly stopped for me;
The carriage held but just ourselves
And Immortality.
Emily Dickinson

Men must endure the going hence,
even as their coming hither.
William Shakespeare

This is a serious game, the defense of one's existence—how to take it away from people and leave them joyous?
Ernest Becker

8
Foreverness

WE SHALL DIE. It is appointed so (Heb 9:27). As Gertrude said to Hamlet, "All that lives must die." Yet we fear the inevitable. A prominent psychologist said that everyone over thirty-five is dominated by the idea that he is going to die.

Death has sometimes been described by mystics as being beautiful. But with no photographs of that realm, we really don't know. The prospects of our new residence frightens us. Hamlet said it well: "Most of us would rather choose those ills we have than to fly to others that we know not of."

We also fear death because it blasphemes life. Macbeth reprimanded the ghost of Banquo, "Do not shake thy gory locks at me." Macbeth suffered guilt from Banquo's assassination, but he also seemed to be shocked that death should attend his royal dinner. After all, there was food and wine; life was beautiful. It was not fair that death should come uninvited to his private party.

Illness grimly reminds us that death is not a state but a process. Katzetnik recounts a physician lancing the knee of a fellow prisoner during the Holocaust. The inmate was so sick that he already resembled a dead man. The doctor "lances and probes into the living flesh, as one probes with a knife point down to the core of a rotten fruit. He scrapes and gouges the scalpel deeper, deeper. When will he hit the bottom? There's no end to it. What is there beyond the swollen rottenness? Is there no bone there at all? Where in the man is the core of life?"[1] There are other times, ironically, when the fear of death is actually replaced by a preference for death. Many suicide notes bear something of this bittersweet desire. Hamlet considered whether to be or not to be. A physician I knew killed himself. He spent his life caring for children with leukemia. As he grew older, he never adjusted to the riddle of a God who loved children and yet created a world with diseases that killed them. Finally, after seeing so many children die, he could no longer face his inadequacy, his inability to heal. Taped to the butt of his shotgun was the short phrase, "It hurts too much to care, and it hurts too much not to care." His grieving life issued in a grieving death.

James Forrestal jumped to his death from his balcony at the Bethesda Naval Hospital. His suicide note was a reflection of the sad lines of Sophocles:

When reason's day sets rayless, joyless
Quenched in cold decay,
It's better to die than linger on and dare
To live when the soul's life is gone.

When life is meaningless and stale, death becomes preferable.

Suicides, like Forrestal's, also see death as a way of successfully dealing with the senselessness of life. This idea from secular existentialism teaches that life and death are endless cycles of meaninglessness. The hero, according to Sartre, is the one who can see the utter futility of life and still choose to go on living. His ideas are immortalized in his play, *No Exit*. Allegedly a tale of hell, it is really a tale of existence and concludes that there is no way out of this jangling and senseless life. The skeptic erroneously believes that death is merely opting out. Death, they say, is followed, not by heaven or hell, but by some kind of eternal bliss that is always better than life is here.

Another view of death, equally agnostic but naively hopeful, teaches that existence alone is the great good. It accepts death grudgingly as the termination of life. Dostoyevsky said that if one even had to stand on a narrow ledge with his face against a cliff for seventy years, it would be better than not to have been at all.

Across the River

A fearful unknown? An escape from life? A foundless hope? Is this death? What is it? What will it be like? Tennyson testifies to our difficulty in defining this realm:

But such a tide as moving seems asleep,
too full for sound and foam . . .

Our imagination is exhausted in trying to describe what our communion with Christ will be like when we do "cross the bar."

We often use Tennyson's metaphor to describe death. Death is frequently seen as a river to be crossed. Legend tells us that Arthur, the King, was taken on a death barge across the murky borders of existence into the fogbound shoals that lay beyond all time. The River Lethe or Styx in Greco-Roman literature saw a lone, hooded figure on a barge taking the dead across the fabled river from this world to the next.

For Christians, the river has always been called the Jordan. This was the final barrier to the Promised Land as Moses and Joshua led the people from the wilderness to the utopia that awaited them. The Jordan River became the symbolic boundary between this world and the next.

When I come to the river at ending of day,
When the last winds of sorrow have blown
There'll be somebody waiting to show me the way
I won't have to cross Jordan alone.

The briefness of this life provides us only the narrowest threshold to eternity. Until this life is completely finished, we cannot speculate on the next. When Ralph Waldo Emerson lay dying, it is said that Parker Pillsbury urged him, at the moment of his passing, to describe what he saw. But when they asked the sage, "What do you see?" Emerson wisely replied, "One world at a time, please!"

Thus, we must be content to wait for eternity. We only create doubt when we use conjecture to pry eternity from the mists. Certainly it is coming. Every word of Scripture seems to confirm it. Heaven is as real as Chicago. Emily Dickinson wrote:

I never spoke with God,
Nor visited in heaven
Yet certain am I of the spot
As if the chart were given.

We survive death. The Bible contains several examples of this. The shade of Samuel the prophet was summoned by the witch at Endor to speak to Saul (1 Sam 28:14). In one of Jesus' parables a rich man, enduring the torments of Hades, pleads for Father Abraham to send the dead Lazarus back to his living brothers (Lk 16:19-31). The apostles saw the walking figure of Christ on the Sea of Galilee and believed him to be a disembodied spirit (Mt 14:26).

Whether life after death exists is not so important a question as the issue of where we shall spend eternity. Those outside of Christ have often told me that they are not afraid of facing death, for in hell they will have lots of company. They have not seen hell as it is: an everlasting night of ultimate aloneness. Those who must go there will not be aware of anyone nearby. The dark intensity of suffering always isolates the sufferer. Hell becomes a vast archipelago of tormented human islands.

Thomas Merton had another view. He believed that the loneliness of hell would come from people being repulsed by the faults in others that they know they also possess:

> Hell is where no one has anything in common with anybody else except for the fact that they all hate one another and cannot get away from one another or from themselves.
>
> They are all thrown together in their fire and each one tries to thrust the others away from him with a huge, impotent hatred. And the reason that they want to be free of one another is not so much that they hate whatever they see in others as they know others hate what they see in them: and all recognize in one another what they detest in themselves: selfishness and impotence, agony, terror, and despair.[2]

Eternity, be it hell or heaven, always begins now. Hell is separation from God and heaven is union with him. Actually, either is merely an extension of the relationship we have with him on earth.

The table in the wilderness is a place of unceasing relationship. Our togetherness with Christ is far more than an intermittent prayer life. Rather, it establishes a strong bridge with two piers, one driven in time and the other in eternity. The trestle of this bridge may be called death.

Paul did not contemplate suicide, but longed for the last glorious state of foreverness. "For me to live is Christ, and to die is gain. If it is to be life in the flesh, that means fruitful labor for me. Yet which I shall choose I cannot tell" (Phil 1:21-22). There is an eagerness about it all. We ourselves ought to be so occupied with Christ that we walk with him, lost in the wonder of our next estate. In the continuum of intimacy with the Savior, we anticipate in joy the boundaries of life. The indwelling presence we received on the day of our conversion makes this hope firm. To be born again is the ultimate answer to death. Death is defeated. For the final separation from life becomes, in Christ, our entrance into glory.

Death has often been compared to birth. If a fetus could reason, he might argue that he did not want to leave the womb. Passing into the birth canal could crush his little form. In the womb his needs are met. He is fed without eating and lives without drawing a breath or having to protect himself from the elements. Life beyond the womb is much less certain.

But birth actually offers new levels of self-awareness and independence. The dark waters of the amniotic refuge are not a haven but a prison. So foreverness in Christ, while it is hidden, offers the promise that life is not destroyed in death but is heightened in every way.

In Christ all is glorious. The communion of the inward table will one day come alive with new reality. The fear of death is displaced as a rock plunged into a pail throws out water. We become free to live in confidence. Jesus' words are realized: "And whoever lives and believes in me shall never die" (Jn 11:26).

Though Jesus prayed in Gethsemane for deliverance from death, he did not quail in terror before it. Apart from the joyous words, "He has risen" (Mk 16:6), the second most meaningful words in the life of Christ must surely be, "Father, into thy hands I commit my spirit!" (Lk 23:46). Our very passing as believers is superintended by the Father of our Lord.

We are as free of death as our resurrected Lord. Death cannot threaten us, for in the very moment of our union with Christ eternal life became ours. Our flesh does not endure and one day must face the end of respiration and pulse. But that moment will come and go and never interrupt the dynamic life that is ours.

A plague once swept the coast of Carthage in North Africa. Everyone feared the contagion so much they shrunk from carrying away the bodies of the dead. But a fearless band of Christians known as the *parabolani* had the courage to do this work. The certain knowledge that death really had lost its sting in the deathless union of believers with their Lord gave them triumph over fear.

In coming to Christ, Christians must take up their cross and welcome their own death to self and ambition. Since it is not possible to die twice, believers, having died ahead of death, are free. Paul said, "I consider that the sufferings of this present time are not worth comparing with the glory that is to be revealed to us" (Rom 8:18). Baptism symbolizes that Christians, by choice, die only once. "The baptized Christian has ceased to belong to the world and is no longer its slave. He belongs to Christ alone, and his relationship with the world is mediated through him. The breach with the world is complete. It demands and produces the death of the old man. In baptism a man dies together with his old world."[3]

Numbering Our Days

We dare not allow the great hope for our resurrection to lull us into spiritual irresponsibility. Our time here is important though brief. Everywhere the Bible says we must be good stewards of our lives. Ephesians 5:16 encourages us to "make the most of the time, because the days are evil." Psalm 90:12 tells us "to number our days that we may get a heart of wisdom." This reminds me of Goya's dark painting, "Saturn Eating His Children." Saturn was the god of time, and time sooner or later devoured all. Omar Khayyám also spoke of time's steady work:

Think in this battered caravanserai
Whose porats are ultimate night and day,
How sultan after sultan with his pomp
Abode his destined hour and went his way.

James asked and then answered the question, "What is your life? For you are a mist that appears for a little time and then vanishes" (Jas 4:14).

In numbering our days, we automatically subtract those already spent from the total number available. Such radical mathematics calls us to consider the priority of those days left to us. What are the events we must give our attention to? To what relationships must we dedicate the remaining years? Jesus made this judgment about the prodigal son, "He . . . took his journey into a far country, and there he squandered his property in loose living" (Lk 15:13). The wasted life throws the days away in worthless pursuits.

When we leave this life, all that will matter is that we prized our relationship with Christ Jesus. I once read of a busy father who at last condescended to give a day of his time to his young son to go fishing. The boy never forgot the day, remembering it to the very hour of his father's death. Since it had been such an important time to the son, he eagerly leafed through his father's diary after the funeral to see what entry his father had made on the great day. He was crestfallen as he read, "The day was lost. . . . I spent it with my son on a fishing trip!" To number our days means we are the stewards of our relationships with others.

Our fellowship at the table is the most important area of the stewardship of our days. A. W. Tozer said that we "who live in this nervous age would be wise to meditate on our lives and our days long and often before the face of God and on the edge of eternity. For we are made for eternity as certainly as we are made for time, and as responsible moral beings we must deal with both."[4]

Companion Spirit

The resurrection created Christianity, but it is sustained and empowered by the constant companionship of the Holy Spirit. Jesus had promised that after he had gone away, he would send the Comforter (Jn 16:7). On Pentecost, the Christ of continuing presence came in the person of the Holy Spirit, who had come as the promise of comfort for those who grieved the absence of the earthly Christ. The Spirit arranges our meetings with Christ at the wilderness table. And when we must leave the closet of this divine fellowship, the beloved Spirit walks with us into the circumstances and struggles of day-to-day living. The same Comforter enables us to deal with our own death.

Perhaps the authenticity of the Spirit's companionship is most appreciated at death. If so, J. C. Pollock's description of the death of Hudson Taylor's second wife is a demonstration of God's faithfulness. The Spirit watched between them with his presence and the assurance that no matter how much pain death brought, the separation was only temporary.

"My hair is so hot!" she said.

"Oh, I will thin it out for you, shall I?" Hudson knew she did not like to have her hair cut short because it could not be done nicely in the Chinese way.

Her hair was matted and tangled with sweat. He began to cut it all off except for an inch of fuzz.

"Would you like a lock of it sent to each of the three children? What message shall I send with it?"

"Yes, and tell them to be sure and be kind to dear Miss Blatchly . . . and . . . and . . . to love Jesus."

When he stopped cutting she put a hand to her head.

"That's what you call thinning out?" she smiled. "Well, I shall have the comfort and you have all the responsibility as to looks. I never do care what anyone else thinks as to my appearance. You know, my darling, I am altogether yours," she said. And she threw her loving arms, so thin, around him and kissed him in her own loving way for it.

Later, as the morning drew on, another conversation between Hudson and Maria began:

"My darling, are you conscious that you are dying?" She replied with evident surprise, "Dying? Do you think so? What makes you think so?"

"I can see it, Darling."

"What is making me die?"

"Your strength is giving way."

"Can it be so? I feel no pain, only weakness."

"Yes, you are going Home. You will soon be with Jesus."

"I am sorry . . ."

"You are not sorry to go to be with Jesus?"

"Oh no!" ("I shall never forget the look she gave me," Hudson later said, "as looking into my eyes she said:")

"It's not that. You know, Darling, that for ten years there has not been a cloud between me and my Saviour." ("I know that what she said was perfectly true.")

"I cannot be sorry to go to Him," she whispered. "But it does grieve me to leave you alone at such a time. Yet . . . He will be with you and meet all your needs."

Soon after nine, the breathing sank lower. Hudson knelt down. With full heart, one of the watches wrote, he committed her to the Lord; thanking Him for having given her and for the twelve and a half years of happiness they had had together; thanking Him, too, for taking her to His own blessed Presence, and solemnly declaring himself anew to His service. . . .[5]

One of these days when our Host rises from the table, we will rise with him and walk with him to our last estate with his Father. It is the final step of victory and union with Christ. The fellowship will be unbroken. Just as it has been at the table, so it will ever be. For our Lord has given us his astounding pledge, "Lo, I am with you always" (Mt 28:20).

Paradise is not a narrow-gated cloister but an open Eden where two—the believer and Christ—may walk abreast into the final presence of God. We who live in fellowship with Christ do not approach this late hour alone.

He is the great rectifier of this human predicament. My mother died on an October day in the late seventies. She had done little more than live for her nine children, and inspired in every one of them a desire to be so much more than any of them could ever have been without her. While I was trying to cut my way through the folderol of funeral preparations, I was also grieving. Death seemed a bleak disinheritance. With little money and magnificent hardship, my mother passed away in anonymity. But my anger at death was soon replaced by the promise of the same Comforter the apostles met at Pentecost.

At his death, D. L. Moody, knowing that same confidence and fueled by the same strong comfort, is reported to have said, "Earth is receding, heaven is descending. This is my coronation day."

Emily Dickinson summoned up her fullest joy and said:

Mine by the right of the white election!
Mine by the royal seal!
Mine by the sign in the scarlet prison
Bars cannot conceal!

Mine, here in vision and in veto!
Mine, by the grave's repeal

Titled, confirmed,—delirious charter!
Mine, while the ages steal!

Death will come, but not unattended. Christ will give us his unfailing presence. We shall rise from the table in the wilderness and sit at the marriage supper of the Lamb. Intimacy will give way to grandeur. And he whom we have met so often will be guest of honor, and all the nations will pay him tribute—and he shall reign forever and ever. Inwardness will be transformed instantly into upwardness. And all the glory of our earthly intimacy with the Savior will be changed to an eternal togetherness indestructable in the heavens.

In the meantime, we wait. Ours is a quiet meal. Our Host sits with us at a table whose silence is the center of our hearts.

Notes

Chapter 1: The Issue of Inwardness

[1]William Shakespeare, *Hamlet,* act 3, scene 4, lines 21-24.

[2]Calvin Miller, *Poems of Protest and Faith* (Grand Rapids, Mich.: Baker, 1965).

[3]Jack Taylor, "Prayer . . . The Priority!" in Ralph W. Neighbour, Jr., comp., *Future Church* (Nashville, Tenn.: Broadman, 1980), p. 80.

[4]Brother Lawrence, *The Practice of the Presence of God* (Mount Vernon, N.Y.: Peter Pauper, 1963), p. 25.

[5]Mother Teresa, quoted in Richard J. Foster, *Meditative Prayer* (Downers Grove, Ill.: InterVarsity Press, 1983), pp. 15-16.

Chapter 2: Barriers to the Inward Journey

[1]Edward Le Joly, *Servant of Love* (San Francisco: Harper & Row, 1977).

[2]T. S. Eliot, "Ash-Wednesday," in *The Waste Land and Other Poems* (New York: Harcourt Brace Jovanovich, 1962), p. 64.

[3]Louis Evely, *That Man Is You,* trans. Edmond Bonin (New York: Paulist, 1963), p. 107.

Chapter 3: The Needle's Eye

[1]John White, *The Golden Cow* (Downers Grove, Ill.: InterVarsity Press, 1979), pp. 47-48.

[2]Carlyle Marney, *Priests to Each Other* (Valley Forge: Judson, 1974), p. 94.

[3]Richard Winston, *Thomas à Becket* (London: Constable, 1967), p. 361, quoted in Eddie Ensley, *Sounds of Wonder* (New York: Paulist, 1977), p. 69.

[4]Louis Evely, *We Are All Brothers* (New York: Doubleday, 1975).

[5]Thomas Edward Brown, "Indwelling," in James Stephens, Edwin L. Beck and Royall H. Snow, eds., *Victorian and Later English Poets* (New York: American Book Co., 1934).

Chapter 4: The Christ of the Table

[1]Sergei Kourdakov, *The Persecutor* (Old Tappan, N.J.: Fleming H. Revell, Spire Books, 1973), pp. 219, 247, quoted in Tom Sine, *The Mustard Seed Conspiracy* (Waco, Tex.: Word, 1981), p. 196.

[2]Dorothy Sayers quoted in Philip Yancey, *Open Windows* (Westchester, Ill.: Crossway, 1982), p. 79.

[3]*Macbeth,* act 5, scene 5, lines 24ff.

[4]Virginia Stem Owens, *And the Trees Clap Their Hands* (Grand Rapids, Mich.: Eerdmans, 1983), pp. 55-56.

[5]John Woolman, *The Journal of John Woolman,* with an introduction by Frederick B. Tolles (Secaucus, N.J.: Citadel, 1961), p. 39.

[6]Paul E. Billheimer, *Don't Waste Your Sorrows* (Fort Washington, Pa.: Christian Literature Crusade, 1977), pp. 82-83.

[7]Giles Fletcher, "He Is," in Phyllis Hobe, ed., *Dawnings: Finding God's Light in the Darkness* (Waco, Tex.: Word, 1981), p. 24.

Chapter 5: Prayer, the Communion of the Table

[1]Donald G. Bloesch, *Faith and Its Counterfeits* (Downers Grove, Ill.: InterVarsity Press, 1981), p. 19.

[2]Taylor, "Prayer . . . The Priority!" p. 79.

[3]Billheimer, *Don't Waste Your Sorrows,* p. 21.

[4]Le Joly, *Servant of Love,* p. 35.

[5]*The Words of Gandhi,* selected by Richard Attenborough (New York: Newmarket Press, 1982), p. 76.

[6]Evely, *That Man Is You,* p. 3.

[7]Brother Lawrence, *The Practice of the Presence of God,* p. 48.

[8]Pascal, *Pensees,* quoted in James W. Sire, *Beginning with God* (Downers Grove, Ill.: InterVarsity Press, 1981), p. 82.

[9]Madame Guyon, *Madame Guyon* (Chicago, Ill.: Moody Press), pp. 41-42.

[10]Earl D. Radmacher, *You and Your Thoughts* (Palm Springs, Calif.: Ronald N. Haynes, 1982), p. 99.

[11]Teilhard de Chardin, quoted in Leo Buscaglia, *Personhood* (New York: Pawcett Columbine, 1982), p. 118.

Chapter 6: The Art of Obedience

[1]Frederick Buechner, *A Room Called Remember* (San Francisco: Harper & Row, 1984), pp. 84-85.

[2]Jean-Pierre de Caussade, *The Sacrament of the Present Moment,* trans. Kitty Muggeridge (San Francisco: Harper & Row, 1982), p. 101.

[3]Bailey E. Smith, *Real Evangelism* (Nashville, Tenn.: Broadman, 1978), p. 57.

[4]Fénelon, *Let Go!* (Springdale, Pa.: Whitaker House, 1973), p. 61.

[5]Ibid., p. 44.

Chapter 7: Widening Our Intimacy with Christ

[1]René Dubos, *Celebrations of Life* (New York: McGraw-Hill, 1981), p. 45.

[2]Owens, *And the Trees Clap Their Hands,* p. 82.

[3]Ibid., p. 138.

Chapter 8: Foreverness

[1]Ka-tzetnik, *House of Dolls,* p. 91, quoted in Irving Halperin, *Messengers from the Dead* (Philadelphia: Westminster), p. 109.

[2]Thomas Merton, *A Thomas Merton Reader,* ed. Thomas P. McDonnell (Garden City, N.Y.: Doubleday, 1974), p. 65.

[3]Dietrich Bonhoeffer, *The Cost of Discipleship* (New York: Macmillan, 1959), p. 257.

[4]A. W. Tozer, *The Knowledge of the Holy* (San Francisco: Harper & Row, 1961), p. 47.

[5]J. C. Pollock, *Hudson Taylor and Maria: Pioneers in China* (Grand Rapids, Mich.: Zondervan, 1970), pp. 205-7.